Byron Kilbourn and Development of Milwaukee

By
Goodwin Berquist
and Paul C. Bowers, Jr.

Published by
The Milwaukee County Historical Society

Sponsored by
Historic Milwaukee, Inc.
Rose Mary & Frank Matusinec
The Harvey E. and Harriette V. Vick Fund,
Greater Milwaukee Foundation

2001

© 2001

ISBN 0-938076-15-9

Library of Congress Card Catalog Number 2001132164

Milwaukee County Historical Society
910 North Old World Third Street
Milwaukee, WI 53203

Printed in the United States of America
Burton & Mayer, Inc.
Brookfield, Wisconsin

Contents

Foreword

Byron Kilbourn was one of the truly remarkable figures of Milwaukee's pioneer years whose accomplishments as a promoter and developer played a significant role in the early history of the State of Wisconsin as well. This in-depth study of Kilbourn's multi-faceted life provides for the general reader and the serious scholar alike new and important insights into the growth and development of both the city and state.

This book also represents a major achievement in Milwaukee historiography. Well written, widely researched, soundly analytical and extensively documented, it stands alone as a serious bio-graphical treatment of one of Milwaukee's pioneer leaders. There are no comparable studies, for example, of his contemporaries, Solomon Juneau and George Walker, nor of any of the other personalities who were important to the political, business and social life of the city in its pre-Civil War years such as Daniel Wells, Alexander Mitchell or Rufus King. As a result this volume contributes a new dimension to our understanding of that formative period of Milwaukee's history as well as to Kilbourn's personal life.

Its broad focus represents local history at its best. Building upon an earlier biography of Kilbourn's father, published by the same authors in 1983 under the title: *The New Eden: James Kilbourne and the Development of Ohio*, this new study of the younger Kilbourn is based upon extensive research which turned up important source material in not only Milwaukee and Wisconsin depositories, but also in distant New England and Ohio, and in Florida where the subject spent his last years.

From this wealth of new information the authors have created a portrait of an individual who was responsible for a number of significant achievements and some controversial failures as well. Kilbourn saw frontier Wisconsin – and its principal city on the shores of Lake Michigan – as an outlet for his dreams and ambitions. As a promoter and developer he was deeply involved in the fields of townsite promotion, land speculation, canal development, railroad construction, harbor improvements, educational endeavors, and a host of related undertakings. He was also actively engaged, with varying degrees of success, in the tumultuous political arena of his time, seeing public office as a logical and necessary complement to his business ventures.

Messrs. Berquist and Bowers are sympathetic to their subject, but not oblivious to his flaws and shortcomings. Unlike some chroniclers of local history who view personalities of an earlier era only from a 20th century perspective, they correctly judge Kilbourn by the standards and practices of his own generation, carefully evaluating his actions against those whom the Milwaukeean competed for public and private advantage.

There is an appropriate timeliness connected with the publication of this volume. Several years ago, through the efforts of some concerned Milwaukeeans, Kilbourn's body was brought back from its original resting place in Florida for reburial here. Public attention generated by this event created a new popular awareness of Byron Kilbourn as one of Milwaukee's founders. This biography, so ably crafted by Goodwin Berquist and Paul Bowers, now offers the opportunity for us to learn in some detail about this fascinating man and the time period in which he accomplished so much towards Milwaukee's early development.

Harry H. Anderson
Milwaukee, Wisconsin

Preface

Milwaukee, Wisconsin became a great city because its citizens were determined to make it so. Three men led the way: Solomon Juneau, a French-Canadian fur trader who settled on the east side, George Walker, a genial Virginian who opened a second trading post on the south side, and Byron Kilbourn, an Ohio canal engineer who developed the land west of the Milwaukee River. Of the three, Kilbourn became the city's foremost promoter. This is his story.

Kilbourn was born in Connecticut at the start of the nineteenth century. He grew up in central Ohio in a community of transplanted New Englanders. His father tried to establish a commercial empire in the Buckeye State. Although he failed in this effort, he provided his son with an example of what might be done in taming the wilderness. James Kilbourn lost a fortune in business reverses after the War of 1812; his son was determined to do better.

Byron's story reads like a romance novel, combining as it does elements of pride and privilege, love and immorality, triumph and tragedy. His name is prominent in the early days of Wisconsin history. He tried to connect Milwaukee by canal with the Mississippi, a dream never realized – though a portion of his waterway provided water power for the city's fledgling industries. It was Kilbourn who established the city's first newspaper and Kilbourn who built the first railroad in the state. He was twice elected Mayor of Milwaukee and came within one vote of being named a U. S. senator.

Despite his accomplishments, Byron's reputation today rests upon the methods he used to win support for a lucrative railroad land grant. Those who stood to profit from his projects thought he could do no wrong; those whose goals differed from his felt he could do nothing but wrong. Throughout Wisconsin the name Kilbourn became a household word; he was admired by some and reviled by others. Few were neutral about this energetic developer who left a conflicting legacy of accomplishment and failure, achievement and infamy.

Our purpose in writing this book was to discover the truth about Byron Kilbourn wherever the truth might lead us. The man we encountered was a complex personality, not easy to judge.

We think you may enjoy learning what we found.

Goodwin Berquist
Paul C. Bowers, Jr.

Acknowledgments

Reconstructing the life of Byron Kilbourn proved to be a formidable challenge. Although a number of Kilbourn's letters regarding business and politics survive, they contain few insights into his private life. Yet it is these details which are the lifeblood of a biography. To be sure, some family letters between Byron and his sisters are housed at the Ohio Historical Center, but they cover only the period of the 1820s and 1830s when Byron was employed as a canal engineer. They tell us nothing about his marriage and family, nor about his later life in Wisconsin. What we needed was new evidence, some document or documents written by one who knew Kilbourn well. We decided to explore the possibility that Byron's first wife, Mary Cowles (a transplanted New Englander), may have written such an account; if so, we hoped that so precious a document, or documents, might still be in existence. A long shot under the best of circumstances!

Mary Cowles was born and raised in Simsbury, Connecticut. Well-educated for a woman of her day, she prepared herself to become a schoolteacher, though she never actually taught. She was a literate, mature woman who in 1826, at age twenty-five, chose to leave the friends and family of her childhood and start life anew in Ohio. She did so at the urging of her older brother, a Worthington, Ohio, businessman who himself moved to Ohio in 1817. We suspected that Mary might be lonely in her new surroundings and might therefore write home frequently. Having no way of knowing for sure whether she did so, we decided to find out.

Our procedure was to contact Archivist Mary Nason of the Simsbury Historical Society. If anyone would know of the existence of some Cowles papers, she would. Mrs. Nason mentioned our inquiry to a co-worker at the Society, and she, in turn, recalled that her friend, Sally Cowles, had just come across such a cache of family letters a week earlier. Sally and her husband, Rollin Cowles, lived in the family homestead in East

Granby (formerly a part of Simsbury) for seventeen years before she decided one day to see what was in some boxes of old letters in the attic. She was so fascinated by what she found that she stayed up until two in the morning reading what Rollin's ancestor had to say!

Contacted by telephone, Sally Cowles confirmed that her husband was the seventh generation Cowles to live at the large house on Spoonville Road, and that she had indeed come across reference to a person named "Byron Kilbourn." In fact, she said, some three dozen such letters existed, a veritable gold mine of new material. Rollin and Sally Cowles generously welcomed us into their home and allowed us to make photocopies of whatever interested us. We are grateful to them for sharing their family letters with us, for it is Mary Cowles' letters from Ohio to Connecticut, and from Wisconsin to Connecticut, which have enabled us to reconstruct the life she and Byron led.

In the process of gathering material for this book, our search has taken us to various libraries and archives where we have uniformly received prompt and helpful service. These repositories include the following: in Connecticut: the Connecticut State Library at Hartford, the Ingraham Memorial Library of the Litchfield Historical Society at Litchfield, and the Simsbury Historical Society Library at Simsbury; in Florida: the Jacksonville Public Library, the Archives of the State of Florida, the Department of Natural Resources of the Division of State Lands at Tallahassee, and the P. K. Yonge Library at the University of Florida at Gainesville; in Maryland: the Maryland Historical Society Library at Baltimore; in Michigan: the Burton Historical Collection of the Detroit Public Library; in New Hampshire: the Baker Library of Dartmouth College, Hanover; in Ohio: Milan Canal Collection at the Milan Historical Museum, Milan, the Ohio Historical Center at Columbus, the Western Reserve Historical Society at Cleveland, and the Worthington Historical Society Library at Worthington; in Wisconsin: Area Research Center at the University of Wisconsin-Milwaukee, the Brown County Central Library at Green Bay, the Kilbourn Public Library at Wisconsin Dells, the Milwaukee County Historical Society Library, the Milwaukee Public Library, the Neville Public Museum in Green Bay, and the State Historical Society of Wisconsin.

We wish to thank the following people for their guidance and help: Harry Anderson, Judy Simonsen, Robert Teske, and Molly Hannan at the Milwaukee County Historical Society, Mary Louise Banzhaf of Milwaukee, Harry Miller, archivist at the State Historical Society of Wisconsin, Paul Woehrmann and Orvil Liljequist of the Milwaukee Public Library, Bruce Hildebrand of Kilbourn Lodge No. 3, Milwaukee, Carol Laun of the Salmon Brook Historical Society in Granby, Connecticut, Betty Guinan, local historian at East Granby, C. H. Harris at the Jacksonville Public Library, John J. Smith, abstracter at the Commonwealth Title Company in Jacksonville, George G. Frederick of Dodge County, Wisconsin, Lois J. Wolf of the Milan Historical Society, Mary Jane Herber, local historian at the Brown County Library, Bud Gussel and Charlotte Walch Davies of Wisconsin Dells, Wisconsin, and Jane Trucksis of the Worthington Historical Society in Ohio.

Three former colleagues at the University of Wisconsin-Milwaukee were particularly helpful: Dr. Reginald Horsman, Emeritus Professor of History, provided an excellent manuscript critique; Dr. Frederick I. Olson, a second historian, supported the project from the beginning of the decade; and Dr. Ralph M. Aderman, a former professor of English, offered helpful editorial comments on the finished manuscript. Former Milwaukee County Historical Society executive director Harry Anderson and Dave Raup of Washington Island provided additional critiques in the latter stages of manuscript preparation.

Special thanks are due Nancy Berquist and Linda Bowers for moral support and helpful suggestions. In a very real sense they have been an important part of Paul's and my effort to bring Byron Kilbourn to life.

Our work on Byron Kilbourn began in 1987. Paul Bowers agreed to tackle the Ohio years (1803-1834). To do so, he spent countless hours laboriously examining the voluminous Ohio Canal Papers at the Ohio Historical Center (many of which have not been examined in decades). He also scrutinized the Micajah Williams Papers on microfilm and discovered many letters involving the plans of the two men for the development of Milwaukee.

Paul died of colon cancer in March of 1998 after a valiant two-year struggle. I am proud to dedicate this book to him.

Goodwin Berquist
Washington Island, Wisconsin
February 1999

Prologue

Early Years. Byron Kilbourn was born in Granby, Connecticut, September 8, 1801, the sixth child and second son of James and Lucy Fitch Kilbourn. James was a man of vision, energy, and determination who left home at age sixteen, penniless and unschooled. He soon found part-time work as a farmhand and became an apprentice clothier. Three years later, by diligence and hard work, he became manager of a textile mill. Tutored by the farmer's son in his spare time, Kilbourn gained a practical education, converted from Congregationalism to Episcopalianism, and ultimately took orders as a deacon in the church. When the fumes of poisonous dyes forced him to leave the clothing industry, he purchased a general store, tavern, and grist mill. By age thirty, he was considered a wealthy man by Granby standards. Byron Kilbourn's mother, Lucy Fitch, was the only daughter of John

James Kilbourn, 1770 – 1850
Byron Kilbourn's father.

Fitch of Windsor, Connecticut, inventor of the world's first successful steamboat. Byron's parents had a deep, tender, and abiding affection for one another.

In James Kilbourn's day, the state of Connecticut was a theocracy run by the Congregationalist Church. Major office holders were invariably of that denomination – a condition that remained in effect until 1818. Further, in the aftermath of the Revolutionary War, Anglicans (or "Episcopalians" as they were later called) were widely considered traitors, since their clergy had remained loyal to the mother church in England during the war. As an Episcopal convert and clergyman, James Kilbourn could either resign himself to verbal abuse and treatment as a second-class citizen or move elsewhere. He chose the latter course.[1]

In the year 1800 James decided to found a new settlement in the west. He planned to establish a community where he and his fellow churchmen could practice their faith in peace and be treated just like their neighbors. It was his father-in-law, John Fitch, who convinced James that the newly opened land west of the Ohio River offered the greatest promise.

Like newcomers to other early communities of Marietta and Cincinnati, Kilbourn's New Englanders planned ahead. First, he and Nathaniel Little made an exploratory trip to the region to choose a suitable site. They selected 16,000 acres straddling the Whetstone River nine miles north of the present-day city of Columbus. By the time the first families arrived in the fall of 1803, town plots were laid out, a gristmill and lumber mill established, cabins erected for temporary housing and community activities, and the first crop harvested. Within a decade of its founding, Worthington, Ohio could boast an Episcopal Church, a Masonic lodge, a respectable academy, and a local newspaper. Dominating the town was James Kilbourn's Worthington Manufacturing Company, a general mercantile firm producing its own wares and dispensing goods brought by wagon train from New York and Baltimore.[2]

Kilbourn also served as a federal district surveyor and land agent. As early as 1805, he began to make plans for laying out the city of Sandusky 120 miles north on Lake Erie. He dreamed of a commercial corridor running south from Lake Erie through Worthington to the Ohio River, a thoroughfare that would connect New York and New Orleans. In furtherance of this goal, James and his oldest son, Hector, laid out a dozen towns in a line north from Worthington to the Great Lake.

Should Sandusky be linked with Portsmouth on the Ohio River, James's assets would rocket in value.[3] In 1807 when Byron was a little over five years old, his mother died in childbirth. With his father and brother constantly away from home, his three older sisters became his surrogate parents. That Byron was the apple of his sisters' eye is apparent by their later correspondence. Although James Kilbourn remarried in 1808, there is no evidence to indicate that Byron and his stepmother were ever close.

What was life like for young Byron as a son of Worthington's first family? For one thing he was well-educated for that day. For seven years he attended school, first the cabin school of Miss Clarissa Thompson, and then the Worthington Academy his father founded. James Kilbourn valued education highly, and he was determined to see to it that the young people of his community should be given a first-class education. The Academy curriculum, and doubtless the

Worthington Manufacturing Company
1818 advertisement.

3

*Worthington's Masonic Temple
built in 1820.*

cabin school, offered basic instruction in spelling, reading, writing, and arithmetic. Geography, history, surveying, navigation, and English comprised the curriculum for secondary students, and advanced students received instruction in Latin, Greek, rhetoric, logic, natural and moral philosophy, and astronomy. Vocal and instrumental music and what today might be called "creative writing" – essays and poetry – completed the studies offered. Compared to other children raised on the frontier in the Old Northwest, Byron Kilbourn was well-educated. Even at the end of the nineteenth century, the average American adult had only five years of schooling.[4]

At age thirteen, Byron was hired as a clerk in his father's company store, a fitting apprenticeship for what James expected to be leadership in a flourishing business. In his off hours, young Kilbourn studied mathematics, history, and law, along with music, of which he was fond. He thought he might become a lawyer one day but his father promptly vetoed that idea. Like many struggling businessmen, James was fed up with being dunned by creditor attorneys in court.

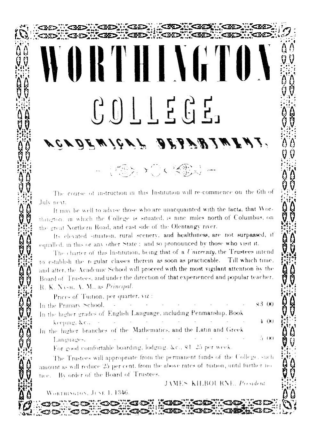

The Worthington Academy
1812 Advertisement.

Byron clearly inherited his father's restless, driving ambition. He had no interest in merchandising, resented the confinement of the store, and yearned to take to the woods as both his father and older brother had. Quite simply, he wanted to strike out on his own. The collapse of the Worthington Manufacturing Company in the aftermath of the War of 1812 gave him his opportunity. At age sixteen, he left home with his father's approval.[5]

Not surprisingly, the occupation he chose was surveying. Ohio offered many opportunities in this field, for there existed countless new towns to be platted and roads to be laid out. As the son of James Kilbourn, even a James Kilbourn financially

5

embarrassed, Byron was well connected. Soon he was busy using his chain and sextant in Marion and Crawford Counties.

Canal Engineer. Hector Kilbourn, Byron's older brother, thought Byron could do better, and he was soon afforded such an opportunity. The state of Ohio was about to undertake one of the great internal improvement projects of the nineteenth century, the building of a canal to link the Ohio River with Lake Erie. The financial panic of 1819, which destroyed Ohio banks and businesses like James Kilbourn's Worthington Manufacturing Company, delayed the process, but by 1822 the Ohio Legislature authorized surveys of five possible routes. Of course, James Kilbourn hoped that the northern terminus of the canal would be at Sandusky, midway between the east and west borders of the state, and that he was about to achieve the commercial prosperity he dreamed of. But it was not to be. The key to the "zig-zag" route finally chosen was political: Ohio's population was concentrated along the Cleveland-Columbus-Portsmouth axis, not the Sandusky-Columbus-Portsmouth route, and the voters who stood to profit directly from the new waterway would be sure to support it. The Sandusky route was rejected also because of insufficient water at Tyamochtee Summit.

Byron sympathized with his father's plans, but he did not hesitate when invited to become a member of the canal corps that would lay out a Cleveland-Columbus canal. To win further voter support for canal building, the residents of the populous Miami Valley were promised a second canal from Cincinnati to Dayton.

The two leaders of Ohio's ambitious canal project were in many ways direct opposites. Micajah Williams of Cincinnati was a Quaker; his cohort, Alfred Kelley from Cleveland, was a Presbyterian. Williams was – with some reservations – a Jackson man; Kelley was a National Republican and Whig. Williams was a migrant to Ohio from the south; Kelley was an eastern addition to the upper crust lawyer-politician-speculator class of the Western Reserve. That two men from such different regions and different political, cultural, and religious backgrounds could work together so closely, so successfully, and for so long is, on first consideration, amazing. But they did so, not only on the public stage, but also on a personal level. They collaborated on land deals; they planned stock options in new banks; and they discussed the sale of waterpower rights along the Ohio Canal. Kelley took a personal and monetary interest in Williams's business masterpiece, the Ohio Life Insurance and Trust Company. Both were nineteenth century liberal capitalists and both believed devoutly in progress and Jeffersonian "happiness" through "development;" that is, making the environment conducive to increased commerce, more extensive farming and service industries, greater trade networks, and more wealth for those who made it happen. Micajah Williams and Alfred Kelley worked together splendidly on the level that was most important to the success of Ohio's canal project. Their world of business and politics was always adventurous and often chaotic. Of these two men, Williams was to play a key role in Byron Kilbourn's Milwaukee career.[6]

Canal records indicate that Byron was hired as "assistant engineer" in September of 1823. He would learn on the job, as would his co-workers. He began in the canal service by marching through forests and slogging through swamps, surveying and plotting a potential canal line. Ultimately, the canal corps set the stage for agreement by the legislature to a two-canal program: one extended from Lake Erie via the Cuyahoga, Tuscarawas, Muskingham, Licking, and Scioto River valleys to the Ohio River; the other ran from Cincinnati northward through the Miami Valley to Dayton. Eventually, this second route extended all the way to the lake at Toledo. The longer "zig-zag" route made Cleveland its northern terminus.

A decisive year for the canal project was 1824. Canal engineers located the basic lines for the two canals, and the stage was set for funding the great work through state bonds. The canal corps – a makeshift and rather hastily cobbled together group in 1823 – grew in number, stabilized, and took on some organizational form while performing remarkably well in the field. As a result of their work, as well as the commissioners' efforts and the subsequent Ohio Canal Act of 1825, administration, finance, and construction of the canal became possible. Byron Kilbourn, who learned on the job in 1823, learned far more in 1824, and established himself as a key member of the field staff. He found, at least for the foreseeable future, an exciting and challenging career.

Acting Commissioner Micajah Williams ordered Byron to make a survey of the proposed reservoir at Licking Summit. This was the first, and most important attempt to solve the problem of providing water for the Muskingham-Scioto route, and it led to the decision to make a "deep cut" as the solution for the water supply at a critical juncture of the canal. Basically, the solution involved constructing a navigable passage through swampland, the area known today as Buckeye Lake. Byron was successful in this endeavor and completed a good year's work in March and April, and, after a brief visit to Columbus, was back on the job in May. When the leader of his crew became ill with rheumatism at Circleville, Byron took his place, completing his assigned duties on time. He was learning how to take command and lead others in pursuit of a common goal. His salary for the 1824 season was $439.50.

Byron worked on both the Ohio Canal and the Miami Canal in 1825. He was placed in charge of locating a lateral branch to Lancaster. In early May, he prepared cost estimates for the Board of Canal Commissioners, which were subsequently approved. Resorting to biblical hyperbole, he predicted a glorious future when "a Big Ditch shall be made, from one extremity of the Empire to the other, on which shall be transported the merchandise of the east, and the rich stuffs of the west. And the ends of the earth shall be brought near, one to the other, and the land be full of gladness."

Byron remained on the Miami Canal through the winter of 1825-26. His rod man was a New York teenager by the name of Increase Lapham, a remarkable young man who would later play a major role in Kilbourn's activities in Milwaukee.[7] As assistant to the resident engineer, Byron participated in assigning contracts and supervised the work on the Middletown-Dayton section of the canal. In 1827 he was himself promoted to the rank of resident engineer and his annual pay was increased to $720. A major portion of his time then involved planning for the construction of locks, bridges, and aqueducts.

Between 1827 and 1833, Byron superintended virtually every aspect of canal construction and maintenance. This included the initial "grubbing and clearing," excavation, embankment, construction of tow paths, locks, culverts and bridges, connection of feeders to the mainline of the canal, maintenance, and repair. His duties fell into four basic categories. First, he checked the work being done by contractors and their laborers on the line. Second, he prepared records of that work (i.e., cost of labor and materials), reporting to either Williams or Kelley. Third, Byron – and probably most of the resident engineers – on occasion had to hire contractors to finish work abandoned or poorly done by the original contractors, even though final authorization for such agreements fell to the two acting commissioners. Finally, in at least one case, Byron appears to have acted as a "constructing" engineer, not merely hiring contractors and overseeing their work, but himself acting as contractor and director of a labor force in the construction of a lime quarry.

Heavy rains and flooding, especially in the winter and spring, interrupted work in progress and ruined work already completed. Water – the lifeblood of the canal – could be and often was a dangerous enemy. The great flood of January 1828, for example, devastated portions of the canal line, but Byron's section was not seriously damaged, and he reported rapid progress on locks and culverts by October.

Byron rode on horseback and often walked the line in the worst of weather. Little wonder that he was sometimes ill with rheumatism, "fevers," and various respiratory ailments. He escaped serious illness, but only for a time. Smallpox and cholera epidemics swept through Ohio during the canal construction years but Byron endured them safely. Initially proud of his strong physique and iron constitution, he eventually suffered from exposure and fatigue, constant companions of all who worked on the canals. In fact, Byron experienced recurrent episodes of rheumatism throughout his life, and it was ill health that ultimately forced him to retire from the canal service in 1833.

All was not always harmonious in the canal service, in part because the line between private interest and public service was not sharply defined. While there is no evidence that Williams or Kelley ever committed an illegal – or even, given the political and economic ethos of the time, questionable – act, they certainly used their powerful positions as acting commissioners to dispense patronage to friends and relatives.

Actual corruption in the form of bribery did exist in the engineering corps, however, and in the spring of 1829, Byron blew the whistle. In June, he wrote Kelley informing him of collusion and bribery involving a fellow engineer. Assuming the mantle of disinterested honesty, Byron observed that "a sense of duty" compelled him to reveal an instance of "cheating," even though this would affect a person who enjoyed Kelley's confidence.

The "collusion" Byron reported involved John Greene and a Mr. Midbury, "partners in taking levels too low of Greene's embankment at Paddy Fork." Five hundred dollars exchanged hands, a considerable amount in that it represented two thirds of a resident engineer's annual salary. Byron claimed he had no self-ish motive in revealing this information, but asserted his unwilling-ness to forfeit Kelley's confidence by withholding it.

He also told Kelley he suspected work on a certain contract on his own line was "in default," had it examined, and was satisfied that it was properly done. Micajah Williams, however, was not so easily satisfied. Sensitive to any hint of abuse of canal funds, given the real control of canal expenditures by the acting commissioners, Williams examined the accounts of work done on Section 99 of Byron's line. When he satisfied himself that there was no "collusion and fraud in the accts." he directed Byron to pay only such claims as were just. Byron seems to have incurred no blame in the Greene-Midbury episode. In fact, he was given added responsibility when a fellow engineer retired from the corps in March 1829.

Byron's health was a matter of constant concern to his family. It is rather remarkable that he avoided serious illness as long as he did, but both he and Alfred Kelley suffered reversals of health in 1832 and 1833. Byron was always touchy regarding any suggestion that he might not be entirely capable of handling any task assigned. When his sisters and father let him know in the summer of 1830 that they were worried about his health, he assured them he was splendidly healthy. In a breezy, joshing style, he chided his sister Laura for obliging him to write yet another letter on the subject of his health. "O, ye of little faith, have ye not the letters that I have written? How much more, then, will you believe me when I say I am well?"

As proof of his condition, Byron cited a trip up the line he had just completed on foot, in two days, from Irrville to Coshocton (about thirty-two miles). "A sick man or one halting with rheumatism cannot do this." "Last Sunday," Byron continued, "I walked from Dresden to this place [Irrville] ... rode to Newark and back the same day and should have liked very well to have gone about 30 miles further ... I was not very sick."[8] Proud and fiercely independent, Byron continued to work effectively until rheumatism forced him to retire in early June 1833. He told Micajah Williams it was his wife, Mary, who compelled him to leave the service.

Heavy rains caused major flooding on Byron's line in the late spring of 1831. On July 30, he reported to Kelley that a breach had opened in the banks of the Licking Summit reservoir. Byron rushed from Newark to organize work on the break and, with the help of a crew of fifteen men was successful. He was concerned that his absence from the summit might be counted as dereliction of duty. He assumed Commissioner Kelley would place the worst construction on his absence. In a letter of August 13, he explained his absence when the breach occurred by citing his work on the South Fork and Granville feeders and a visit to check the Stillwater locks, all tasks previously assigned by Kelley. Kelley fired the superintendent of the reservoir and quickly calmed Byron's ruffled feelings.

The breach crisis may have contributed to Byron's decision to leave the canal service. At any rate, he seems to have determined by early 1831 to resign his position as resident engineer. Time and circumstance confirmed that decision. By October of 1832, the last leg of the main canal to the Ohio River at Portsmouth was completed.

Byron's decision to retire from the canal service may also have been hastened by a devastating Ohio River flood – the greatest in memory – in the winter of 1832. Then, too, Commissioners Williams and Kelley were contemplating their departure from the service. When Williams received a federal appointment as surveyor general of the Northwest Territory by President Andrew Jackson in March of 1831, he informed the Ohio Legislature that he would resign from his post as soon as an adequate replacement could be found.

Looking toward the future, Byron suggested to the president of the Canal Commission that he establish a collector's office at Lockbourne at the mouth of the Columbus feeder. He pointed out that an office there would be conveniently situated halfway between Chillicothe and Newark. Further, he had no doubt that considerable hydraulic power could be created at Lockbourne which, with business emanating from the surrounding country, would produce a boom economy. Byron went on to note that he had "purchased a small interest at this place," Lockbourne, and proposed, "if I can make suitable arrangements, to settle there as soon as the canal line south of Licking Summit is completed and a member of the corps is released to take my place north of the summit." Should the Canal Board establish an office at the mouth of the Columbus feeder, "I would respectfully solicit the appointment of Collector."[9]

As one of Ohio's first canal engineers, and one who had been given considerable responsibility, Byron had reason to expect favorable consideration for this or any other collectorship. He thought he had a special relationship with Micajah Williams, and perhaps he did. But he did not take into account Williams' political pragmatism. A novice when it came to politics, Byron never had a chance at gaining the position he sought.

Micajah Williams was a Jackson man but not rigidly ideological. He supported the Democratic Party nationally, regionally, and socially, insofar as the party was in turn useful in local, state and regional development. Kilbourn learned from Williams that getting things done in the political arena required political activity and savvy. But he never learned how to delegate authority effectively – an art at which Williams was a master. Byron was the kind of authoritarian leader who simply had to control things. Later, in Wisconsin, he was rarely able to create an effective cadre of supporters to carry out his canal and railroad plans.

In August of 1831, Williams broached the subject of Byron's participating in territorial surveys west of Lake Michigan. Byron replied that he would like to join the project. More than likely Williams laid out for Byron his plan to appoint a hand-picked group of surveyors who would seek out promising town sites for purchase. At the heart of this land speculation scheme was the plan to locate a site for a major port city on the western shore of Lake Michigan.

Five months later, Byron changed his mind. "On more full and deliberate consideration," he wrote Williams, "after having obtained the sense of my wife on the subject, I have concluded to decline it entirely. My reasons are ... the pain and solicitude it would occasion her, and the delay that will probably take place in ordering the surveys." (A treaty granting the government title to southeastern Wisconsin was not signed with resident tribes until 1833.) Byron thought he could make a living for himself and his family "with less exposure" close to home. "I shall fix my residence at Columbus," he said.[10]

Williams was the one man in the world Byron most admired, respected, and trusted. At the time, the two had been acquainted for eight years, and Byron apparently hoped for and expected some help from this man in getting some of the positions he now sought. He miscalculated. Williams had his own agenda, and he made it clear that Byron fit into his schemes as a surveyor in the Michigan Territory, not as a jack-of-all-trades in central Ohio. Byron did receive an appointment as city engineer and surveyor of Columbus in 1832, but these two jobs combined did not bring the salary expected. Meanwhile, his health continued to deteriorate.

By July of 1832, Kilbourn was essentially unemployed, "not doing much at present, except doctoring himself for the rheumatism." His wife, Mary, reported that if he regained his health he "thinks himself destined for the West." The following January the family was living in a kind of limbo with no clear or settled direction for the future. Byron had sold his farm on the Muskingham River and his property at Lockbourne and Sandusky, but the proceeds were not sufficient to guarantee him a life of independence.[11]

A year to the day after he wrote Williams rejecting his appointment of a surveyorship, Byron wrote his old mentor again, coming as close as he ever did in his adult life to pleading for a favor. Although still ill with rheumatism, he was desperate for a job, and Williams' original offer must have seemed to him his best hope. Byron – who later in life was described as independent, proud, even arrogant and domineering, and who could not abide abasing himself or suffering even the appearance of condescension – must have found writing this letter to his professional mentor, to whom he wished to appear the very model of self-reliance, near torture.

He began his letter by observing that he was "troubling" Williams on this subject – that is, his application for an appointment as a surveyor in the territory under Williams' purview – and asked to be excused for a request that might seem "importunate." He reminded Williams of his abilities in the field, and then addressed an issue Williams had broached earlier – Byron's ignorance of political realities. Rather self-righteously, Kilbourn claimed that hard work and positive results were far more important than political connections.

Nonetheless, he did understand that the "right" political connections were essential to anyone who sought a career in the public arena. He knew Williams' support was essential, that Williams was in fact his one truly important political connection. Although he was surely sincere in his expression of thanks for Williams' backing over the years, Byron, on a deeper level, resented being beholden to any man.

He said he realized "political sentiments" might play a role in Williams' appointments, "but have indulged the hope that you would not bring it to bear in my case...." Byron indicated that he opposed President Andrew Jackson's stand on the tariff and the Supreme Court, but he "thought most, if not all, the other measures of his administration well calculated to sustain the interests of the country." He was not a supporter of Henry Clay, the presidential nominee of the National Republicans, fearing that he would concentrate too much power in the hands of the chief executive. He favored Jackson's plan to distribute surplus federal funds to state banks, thereby undercutting the power of the Bank of the United States. In short, Byron seemed to base his political affiliation on "the lesser of two evils."

Reading all this, one might suspect the politically canny Williams concluded that Kilbourn had not thought through the ramifications of politics local, state, and regional. Perhaps like his father before him, Byron deluded himself into thinking he could do everything alone. Ultimately, politics for him became a means to an end, a method of gaining support for his projects, rather than a matter of furthering a set of political principles.

In the final paragraph of his letter, Kilbourn came perhaps as close as he ever did to pleading: "I am induced to press this subject more than I otherwise should do, from a feeling of almost necessity...." He swallowed his pride, admitted that he was not entitled to special consideration, and acknowledged that there were others whose "services and talents would rank far beyond mine...." But "my prospects here are not very flattering, and the wish I have for active employment" is not likely to be realized in "this section of the Country."[12] Accordingly, Williams appointed Kilbourn, along with several others, to positions as district surveyors in that part of the Michigan Territory west of the Lake that later became the state of Wisconsin.

Kilbourn's appointment was not made official until the spring of 1834. In the interim, he found employment as engineer for the Milan ship canal, one of many local canal projects that proliferated during the Ohio Canal era. Milan was a small village in Huron County near Lake Erie, thirteen miles southeast of Sandusky. The shortest of Ohio's canals, only three miles long, the waterway connected Milan basin with Fries Landing, a point on the Huron River from which the river was navigable out into Lake Erie. The Milan canal was built so that Ohio farmers could ship their wheat to the east. By 1847, the town had become second in the world only to the Russian port of Odessa in wheat exports.

It may have been Alfred Kelley who recommended Kilbourn for this position. Kilbourn worked on the canal for nine months as an engineer, its only engineer, in fact. A canal ledger entry indicates that he was employed between July 1, 1833, and April 1, 1834, and that he received a salary for this period of $788.58.[13] Construction of the canal was suspended in 1834-35 due to a lack of funds and a sharp drop in grain prices.

Courtship and Marriage. Beginning in 1823, Byron Kilbourn led the nomadic life of a canal engineer. Single, self-confident, robust, and ambitious, he more than likely attracted the attention of some members of the opposite sex. Certainly his letters to his sisters indicate he found many women attractive. While the evidence is sketchy, sometime between his leaving his father's business in 1817 and his marriage to Mary Cowles in 1827, Byron precipitated a family crisis by apparently fathering a child out of wedlock. His sister, Harriet Buttles, delicately put the matter this way in a family letter: "nothing more transpired respecting Byron's unfortunate affair. I believe Pa has written him to come home but I sincerely hope he will not. Mr. B. [Harriet's husband] says they cannot get him unless he chooses to come." [14]

The nature of the scandal is clear: Byron Kilbourn, a member of Worthington's first family, was presumed to be the father of an illegitimate child. Harriet went on to recommend that the family "wait and see what proof there may be, and whether the little unfortunate bears any resemblance where by the truth may be ascertained." Note that Harriet's letter does not say the "little unfortunate" *was* Byron's child. Perhaps it was not, or could not be proved to be. Whatever the facts of the case, Byron himself never mentioned the matter in any of his letters which survive. We do know, however, that as he approached age twenty-five he began to think seriously about getting married and settling down. Many of his Worthington friends had already done so and he began to wonder if his opportunity would ever come. It was at this point that he met Mary Cowles of Simsbury, Connecticut, the sister of one of his brothers-in-law, Rensselaer Cowles.

Rensselaer emigrated to Worthington in 1817, part of the postwar migration of New Englanders seeking new economic opportunities in the west. Women came too, no doubt many with their husbands and families, but others seeking just those things. And perhaps something else, too – some unidentified, yet strongly desired way *out* of a constricting and stultifying existence and *into* a life of greater freedom and happiness. Mary Cowles was one such seeker – unmarried, well-educated for the day, loved by her father, stepmother, brothers, and sisters.[15] Her family cherished her and her parents financed her schooling well into her twenties.

When Mary was twelve, she began a cycle of visitation to the homes of family members – aunts, uncles, cousins, grandmother. She wrote from her grandmother's home in Rome, New York, pleading with her father to write to her and entreating him to let her come home soon. Seven years later, having been brought by her father to his brother's home in Southington, Connecticut, Mary found herself left to attend a mentally disturbed cousin. It was a distressing experience for Mary, who was probably herself experiencing the painful passage from adolescence to woman-hood at the time. Unmarried but with a strong wish to start a family of her own, Mary longed for self-fulfillment.

Her older brother, Rensselaer, suggested her opportunities for finding a husband might be better in Ohio than in her home state. And so in 1826 she set out westward, anxious but excited and hopeful. Mary's decision to leave family and childhood friends may have received some spark from Byron's father, Colonel James Kilbourn, whom she met at Rome. The Colonel had returned east to rally support for his failing economic fortunes in Ohio, and as ever, he ebulliently boosted the marvelous opportunities awaiting those who migrated to the western country. Far more decisive was the example and influence of her trusted older brother, Rensselaer. He had married into the Kilbourn clan in 1818 and was much taken with the political and economic views of his father-in-law for the development of central Ohio.

Upon her arrival in Ohio, Mary discovered she missed her family very much. Still in many ways an adolescent – timid, unsure, dependent – though at an age that (as Rensselaer pointed out) would not admit of it, she now in Worthington virtually reproduced her Connecticut situation, with this difference: women not men dominated her life until her marriage to Byron. The Kilbourn family – a close-knit clan of sisters – enfolded her. James Kilbourn may have been the patriarch of the clan but his daughters provided the very warp and woof of its existence and character. Their deep religious piety, kindness, sharing, and supportive spirit, strong roots in the community, sensibility of sacrifice for the good of those they loved, drew her close within the circle of the Kilbourns and their society.

For a while Mary looked for a teaching position. Several were available, and with her educational training and the support of the Kilbourns, she surely could have secured such a post. But her search was desultory; marriage was her real goal. She sewed, visited – mostly within the Kilbourn family network – went to church. When her younger stepbrother, Sylvester Dering Cowles (called "Dering" by the family), followed Mary to Worthington, he "kept bar" at James Kilbourn's hotel for a "few weeks" at the patriarch's request. Dering later worked in the Kilbourn company store that Rensselaer managed. Neither Rensselaer nor Mary seemed to have been concerned that their younger brother might be corrupted by tending bar at "Kilbourn Central." It was, after all, in the family.

When Mary and Byron met, they may have been strangers, but they were also, more importantly, family. That of course did not mean they were destined to be married. But given the situation and aims of each at the time they met, the confluence of personal, social, and economic desires and family and social pressures, one would be bemused, if not surprised, had they not gotten married. Exactly when, where, and under what circumstances the two met is not recorded in extant family correspondence. Surely the Kilbourn sisters – Lucy, Harriet, Laura, and Orrel – had much to do with their meeting, if they did not actually arrange it. Perhaps Rensselaer, married to Laura, played a role. He had, after all, hinted rather broadly that Ohio would prove a better place than Connecticut for Mary to find a husband.

Byron was still working on the Miami Canal when he first met Mary, but by the time he wrote Whitfield Cowles to obtain permission for the union, he had been promoted to resident engineer on the Ohio Canal. He therefore believed himself to be in a promising position to sue for Mary's hand. Just as clearly he believed that winning the approval of Mary's father was no perfunctory matter. In the summer of 1827, just a little less than a year after Mary arrived in Worthington, Byron wrote to Whitfield Cowles asking a father's blessing on the marriage of his daughter to a man who, though personally a stranger, was one of the "family."

The language and tone of Byron's letter reveal a man who had shed the image of the carefree and callow swain of the canal circuit. Byron – keenly intelligent, enormously energetic, determined, calculating – was no longer a boy; in fact, no longer "young." He chose a new persona, and marriage to an impeccable partner was important, indeed necessary, to complete his metamorphosis.

Mary was no blooming Venus, being eight months older than Byron and on the cusp of spinsterhood. Deeply emotional, her religious experiences, especially in the revivalist atmosphere of early nineteenth century New York, seem to have exacerbated her feelings of inadequacy and dependence on others for sustenance, guidance, approval, safety, and fulfillment. Her letters to family members are filled with self-abnegation, anxiety, and pleas for support. But Mary also possessed a sense of her own worth, intelligence, and imagination. She had been coddled through life, surrounded by friends and family, and was thus unprepared for Byron's frequent absence on canal business.

Perhaps not surprisingly Mary felt different from and superior to the society she found at Worthington. She returned the Kilbourn sisters' enveloping support with admiration and affection. Later, as a "canal wife," she depended on them when she or her children were sick or otherwise in need, and they did not fail her. But although she admired and trusted them, Mary found the Kilbourn sisterhood lacking in independent spirit, inquiry, learning, and reach of mind. She worried about her daughters' future and came to believe that education for them was more important than for males. Mary was not a silly, weak, vaporous creature, nor was she merely passive.

Byron decided to marry after a good deal of soul searching. Did Mary experience doubts and uncertainty as her marriage day approached? Her contemporary, Harriet Beecher, a New Englander who also migrated to Ohio, viewed her own approaching nuptials with bemusement if not trepidation. In 1836 she confided to her friend Georgina May that "about an hour more and your old friend, companion, schoolmate, sister, etc. will cease to be Hattie Beecher, and change to nobody knows who."[16] A half hour later she married Professor Calvin Stowe, a member of the faculty of the Lane

Theological Seminary in Cincinnati. Mary's letters reveal no fear of being swallowed up or "de-personed" by marriage and a male-dominated life. Both Mary and Byron wanted to get married for reasons complex, social, and personal; each different but decisive and intersecting.

If Mary had reservations about marrying a canal engineer, she may have caught it from her father. Of all the family – Cowles and Kilbourns – only Whitfield remained cool to the marriage. He may have heard about the unfortunate child episode. Perhaps he was concerned about the life his daughter would face in the rough, lonely interior of Ohio. If so, he was prescient, for that life ultimately killed Mary, destroying her spirit and body.

Byron made up his mind. He was going to marry Mary Cowles. Once he chose a course of action he was hard to deflect. Yet he felt it necessary to ask by letter for Whitfield Cowles' blessing on the marriage. This was not mere custom or good form. Byron recognized that this was a Connecticut clan concern, a family affair. He sought the manner of gentility, the tone and language of a gentleman and a member of the tribe. Deference and assertiveness ebb and swell throughout his letter, but it is obvious that he meant to address Cowles man to man, peer to peer, as well as suitor of his daughter's hand in marriage.

Byron's letter, dated July 25, 1827, is the cleanest, most legible letter he ever wrote. The lines go straight across the page, shading very slightly upward as they proceed, letters and words carefully made. One gets the impression that he worked long and hard to produce a final draft. He began by introducing himself as "the son of an ancient friend." James Kilbourn was well-known throughout the Simsbury-Granby area as a successful businessman, a leader of immigration to Ohio, and a tireless booster of the new west. Thus, Byron was not a complete stranger to Mary's father but a New Englander born with roots in central Connecticut reaching back over a century. Byron's tone was that of a mature, self-confident adult. He confessed his love for Mary and eased Cowles' concern about the lack of a dowry. He admitted that his canal duties kept him away from home much of the time and he spoke fondly of visiting friends and relatives with Mary whenever time permitted.[17]

Kilbourn's letter is practical, businesslike, and informative. With pardonable understatement he acknowledged that "it would no doubt be satisfactory to know something of my person and prospects before deciding on a subject of such moment, but my own testimony might not perhaps be the most acceptable." Instead, Byron referred to Mary and her brother Rensselaer as his advocates. He declared his prospects for the future were "tolerably flattering;" he had just been promoted to resident engineer, and the construction phase of the canal project was likely to take several more years. Health, hard work, and thrift were Byron's first concerns; "in the western country these are the surest passports to independence." Whatever reservations Mary's father may have had about the match, he gave his consent. Byron and Mary were married at St. John's Episcopal Church in Worthington December 25, 1827.

If Mary had reservations about the union, they probably stemmed from Byron's being so often away on canal business. Frequently lonely and some of the time in poor health, Mary bared her soul in her letters home. As she wrote her parents in February of 1828, Byron was "absent from me at this time of the year for 5 days at a time in every other week and, as soon as spring opens, the busy operations of his line will require his attendance as many days of every week." The Kilbourn family network (female nurture and support division) sought to keep Mary centered on the positive aspects of her new life. Byron's younger sister, Orrel, came to visit in the summer, providing welcome relief from loneliness and, later, the incessant demands of child rearing. Mary assured her parents that "I have everything that I wish ease, leisure and an affectionate husband can give me or procure with money." With evident satisfaction, she noted that Byron "tells me that he has heard that there are two kinds of wives, one that asks too much and one that asks not enough; he thinks I am one of the latter kind." Never one to underestimate earthly life as a vale of trial and tears, Mary added, "If I am such now, in his eyes, I may not always appear so to him at different times, or see with different eyes, or rather different feelings."[18]

She found "Mr. Kilbourn to be a man of more than usual candour, and a fine disposition; at present we are happy together, time alone will discover whether we shall be thus until death do us part; my continual prayer is that I may have wisdom and understanding to fulfill all duties acceptable to my husband and my God." Because of Byron's frequent transfers, Mary's dream of a home of her own had to wait, and when it at last was within Byron's grasp, it came only months before her early death at thirty-six.

As we noted earlier, illness from exposure was a common experience for canal workers. What we have not mentioned is the absence of medical care for their wives and families, marooned in dusty canal hamlets. Mary traveled from her temporary home by the canal to Worthington to bear her first child, Glorianna Havens, in 1829. Her second, Lucy Fitch, arrived after a difficult birth in 1831. Her letters to relatives in Connecticut document the weakness of her constitution. She often felt unwell, despite the loving care of Byron's sisters and the medical advice of Dr. Jones, a family relative and physician at Worthington.

While Byron poured his time and energy into the myriad demands of his job, Mary's contentment with her marriage was rather quickly strained. If, as she claimed, Byron's society was all that she needed to be happy, she found the canal to be a demanding rival. In April of 1828, she informed her parents that "Mr. Kilbourn left me, 3 days since. I expect him home this afternoon. I am very lonely during the time he is absent, which at this season amounts to about half of the time." Mary added that she was constantly "thinking of you all; of our house – door yard and gardens. I yearn," she wrote, "to fly to you. I often see Papa in my dreams. I am as much of a Baby for Papa and Momma as ever. Oh! if Papa could come and see us this summer, it would do us more good than you could imagine. I sometimes think it necessary to my happiness." Papa, however, never came.

Mary complained of the excessive heat of an Ohio summer, which she especially felt during her first pregnancy. Her discomfort notwithstanding, Byron dutifully announced the birth of Glorianna Havens on November 23. The baby, he wrote his father-in-law, was "plump, fat and healthy" and Mary was doing well.

He neglected to mention that his wife had been quite ill. Mary suffered from severe colds and attendant fatigue. Ultimately, she appears to have contracted tuberculosis. When illness struck, Byron and Mary did not at first return to Worthington. Instead they brought Worthington to them, in the person of Orrel. "We are in quite a pickle," Byron wrote Orrel May 2,1830; "Mary weaned her child a week or two since, and thought that she would be able to get on very easy," but "Glorianna was scarcely weaned when she got a diarrhea" which made it more laborious to take care of her. Being up nightly fatigued her, and Mary was "now too unwell to take care of herself & child." For his part, Byron wrote, business "requires me to be absent most of the time."[19]

Mary recovered but was soon pregnant with a second child. The birth of Lucy Fitch was difficult, and both mother and daughter were dangerously ill for some time. Indeed, Mary never fully recovered her health thereafter, suffering from various debilitating illnesses until she finally succumbed to pneumonia in 1837.

Mary Cowles loved Byron Kilbourn and had a genuine concern about her daughters' education. Never in good health after the birth of Lucy Fitch, Mary desired above all else to start a home of her own, an impossibility when Byron was constantly on the move with canal business. In spite of frequent illness, she decided to head west with her husband rather than remain amongst the Kilbourn clan in Worthington or to return to her ancestral home in Connecticut. Mary was a realist: she knew Byron was addicted to "getting ahead" and that business would always be his first concern. Better to be with the man she loved than rely upon occasional letters to replace an absentee husband.

Endnotes

[1] For a detailed account of James Kilbourne's life see Goodwin Berquist and Paul C. Bowers, Jr., *The New Eden: James Kilbourne and the Development of Ohio* (Lanham, Md.: University Press of America, 1983, 2001); see also Paul C. Bowers, Jr., and Goodwin F. Berquist, Jr., "Worthington, Ohio: James Kilbourne's Episcopal Haven on the Western Frontier," *Ohio History*, 85, No. 3 (Summer 1976), 249-258. The family name is sometimes spelled Kilbourn or Kilbourne. James preferred to add the "e" but since Byron did not, that is the form used in references to him throughout this work.

[2] Berquist and Bowers, *The New Eden*, pp. 35-84, 270. A comprehensive treatment of the community James founded is presented by Virginia E. McCormick and Robert W. McCormick, *New Englanders on the Ohio Frontier: Migration and Settlement of Worthington, Ohio* (Kent, Ohio.: Kent State University Press, 1998). The Worthington Manufacturing Company, its branches and diverse activities, are described in *The New Eden* pp. 115-119, *passim*.

[3] James Kilbourne's "Sandusky Enterprise" is described in *The New Eden*, pp. 151-165.

[4] Todd Brewster and Peter Jennings, *The Century* (New York: Doubleday, 1998), p. 16.

[5] *The New Eden*, pp. 61-62. See also Kilbourn Family Papers, Ohio Historical Center, Columbus (hereafter referred to as OHC), and Byron Kilbourn's Address to the Kilbourn Historical and Genealogical Society, State Historical Society of Wisconsin, Madison (hereafter referred to as SHSW), microfiche of the Kilbourn Historical and Genealogical Proceedings, 1854, 16 pp. At the time Byron was honorary president of the society; his remarks were read aloud to members in his absence on August 20, 1854. Payne Kenyon Kilbourn, *The History and Antiquities of the Name and Family of Kilbourn* (New Haven, Conn.: Durrie and Peck, 1856), pp. 232-248.

[6] The Ohio Canal Papers and Canal Commissioners' Correspondence are housed at OHC. This summary of Byron Kilbourn's experience as a canal engineer is based upon a careful study of these sources and an examination of the letters his wife, Mary, sent back to Connecticut. Cowles Family Papers, privately held by the Cowles family of East Granby, Connecticut. For a sketch of Williams's business activities, see Harry N. Scheiber, "Entrepreneurship and Western Development: The Case of Micajah T. Williams," *Business History Review* (Winter 1963), pp. 345-368. For Alfred Kelley, see Scheiber, "Alfred Kelley and the Ohio Business Elite, 1822-1859," *Ohio History*, 87, No. 4 (Autumn 1978), 365-392.

[7] Byron Kilbourn to Aurora Buttles, May 8, 1825, "Thirteen Letters," SHSW;

autobiographical letter, Increase Lapham to Lyman C. Draper, May 16, 1859, SHSW.

[8] Byron Kilbourn to Laura Kilbourn Matthews, May 8 [1830?], Irrville, Ohio, SHSW, File 1825.

[9] Byron Kilbourn to the president and board of Canal Commissioners, January 20, 1831, Canal Commissioners' Correspondence, OHC, Microfilm Reel 4.

[10] Byron Kilbourn to Micajah Williams, January 23, 1832, OHC. Williams Papers, Microfilm Reel 2.

[11] Cowles Family Papers.

[12] Byron Kilbourn to Micajah Williams, January 23, 1833, OHC, Williams Papers, Microfilm Reel 2.

[13] Ledger in Milan Canal Papers, Milan Historical Museum, Milan, Ohio.

[14] Harriet Kilbourn Buttles to Orrel Kilbourn, June 29, n.d., OHC, Buttles Family Papers, Manuscript 951. This letter was probably written between 1821 and 1822.

[15] For this and other details of Mary's life, see Cowles Family Papers.

[16] Harriet Beecher to Georgiana May, January 6, 1836, quoted in Jeanne Boylston, Mary Kelley, and Ann Margolis, eds., *The Limits of Sisterhood: They Became Sisters on Women's Rights and Women's Sphere* (Chapel Hill: University of North Carolina Press, 1988, paperback edition), p. 2.

[17] See Mary's letters to her family in Connecticut, 1828-1832, Cowles Family Papers.

[18] Mary Cowles Kilbourn to Whitfield Cowles, April 23, 1828, Cowles Family Papers.

[19] Byron Kilbourn to Orrel Kilbourn, May 2,1830, OHC, Kilbourn Family Papers, Mss. 332, VFM 328.

Kilbourntown

Byron Kilbourn proceeded to Green Bay by boat, the fastest mode of transportation available to him, arriving May 8, 1834. Green Bay was the oldest community in the territory, having been founded two centuries earlier by French explorer Jean Nicolet. A frontier fort and trading post populated by a hundred people, mostly French-Canadian, the village served as a supply base for all who entered the region. Here Byron purchased what he needed to begin surveying. His assignment was twofold: to lay out townships in what would later become Manitowoc County and to identify the most promising site on the western shore of Lake Michigan for a major commercial port.

In the ten months that followed, Byron laid out fifteen townships. The task proved to be more difficult than he expected, even for an experienced surveyor like himself, as he explained in a September letter to his employer Micajah Williams.

> For some years past I have been more or less afflicted with rheumatism & some instances of which you have witnessed – On making up my mind to Come to the N.W. Ter. I had some doubts on this head, which was also strongly urged by my family, but the prospect was too tempting – I had heard the Country uniformly represented as of the first order, and desired much to make at least one visit to it – In fine I decided to undertake a job of surveying, believing that in a fine country and a healthy atmosphere I should be no more liable to rheumatic attacks, than at home in ordinary occupations nor do I yet think I should, if my district were as good as the greater part of the purchased Country is represented to be – But should my district throughout be as bad as the Tps. run, I think I hazard but little in supposing that an equal

amount of unfavourable country *for the Surveyor* cannot easily be found – the excessive fatigue of traversing Cedar Swamps – sinking through their mossy surface into the water & mud, clambering over a continual series of fallen trunks as craggy as a hedge, or creeping through thickets of the closest kind, the profuse perspiration consequent upon such exertions in warm weather, added to the continual wetness of the feet & legs – is what should only be undertaken and executed by a constitution of iron.

Quite an admission considering Byron's earlier pride in his own good health and his only recent recovery from a prolonged illness. "Laboring under the withering influence of rheumatism," Byron was determined to succeed. Added to this tale of physical woe was the high cost of transporting supplies overland from Green Bay. "I am no friend to hard labour without adequate compensation," Kilbourn told Williams; nonetheless he lost money as a surveyor in the Manitowoc country, and his career in this line was short-lived, ending in March of 1835.

Artist's conception of Solomon Juneau's Trading Post.

Despite recurring bouts of illness, Byron found the time and energy to explore widely in the new territory. Between the Manitowoc region to the north and the border of the state of Illinois to the south lay 120 miles of wilderness. A fur trader's post on the Milwaukee River was the only white habitation between these two points; settlements in the rest of the territory consisted of a small mining community at Mineral Point and military posts at Portage and Prairie du Chien. In 1831, the first of two important Indian treaties was signed, opening up southeast Wisconsin for white settlement. Major S.C. Stambough explored the newly opened territory for the federal government. He reported that the Milwaukee River offered fine opportunities for mill sites and that the surrounding country contained "attractions to the agriculturalist rarely to be found in any country."[1] Speculators immediately took note.

Among them was a young Yankee lawyer from Green Bay named Morgan Lewis Martin. A graduate of Hamilton College, Martin had moved from upstate New York to Detroit. Then at the suggestion of his cousin, James Duane Doty, the territorial judge, he had headed farther west to Green Bay. As was customary among speculators of the day, Martin needed financial backing to purchase promising town sites. Consequently, early in 1833, he entered into a partnership with Michael Dousman of Mackinaw City. On the lookout for attractive property, Martin made his first visit to the mouth of the Milwaukee River in June. He hoped to meet Solomon Juneau there, but Juneau was in Chicago on business. Martin drew a map of the area, and the following October he and Juneau joined forces. For a fee of $500 and a handshake, Martin became half owner of Juneau's considerable claim in the area. The partnership proved to be mutually profitable. As an elected representative in the Michigan Territorial Legislature, Martin had valuable political contacts in Detroit, along with financial ones back east; he provided money and timely political advice. Juneau possessed important property rights and dealt with prospective buyers at the site. Together the two planned to develop a new town.[2]

*Solomon Juneau, Milwaukee's
first permanent white settler.*

The winter of 1833-34 brought a temporary halt to speculative activities in the Milwaukee area, but in March, a genial Virginian by the name of George Walker appeared on the scene. Twenty-three years old at the time (younger than either Juneau or Kilbourn), Walker established another trading post on Milwaukee's south side. Although he built a cabin and store, he did not own the land on which they were located – a practice known as "squatting" – and this fact would prevent him from becoming a major force in Milwaukee development for some years. The area where he settled became known as Walker's Point. Walker secured goods for trade with the Indians from Chicago. In the years that followed, he became a popular local figure, twice elected Mayor of Milwaukee after serving as alderman. Walker's business interests included state and local railroads. He played a key role in securing a soldiers' home for Milwaukee after the Civil War. An immense man physically, Walker was among Milwaukee's most popular figures. Along with Juneau and Kilbourn, he eventually became one of the city's three founding fathers.[3]

Byron Kilbourn's first view of Milwaukee occurred in November 1834. At the end of the surveying season, he rode south to see for himself what the Milwaukee area had to offer. What he found more than met his expectations. The woods about the mouth of the Milwaukee River gave promise of plentiful material for fuel and building. There was maple, birch, hickory, beech, walnut, pine, sycamore, hackberry, poplar, aspen, basswood, and four different kinds of oak. Wildlife flourished: geese, ducks, and pigeons so numerous you could snare them with hoop nets as they flew by. There were elk, deer, wolves, raccoons, prairie hens, partridge, wild turkey, rabbits, and squirrels beyond counting. Early settlers would have

Morgan L. Martin

no trouble securing building supplies or meat for the table. The banks of the Milwaukee River were full of life, too. There was mink and muskrat for trapping, crabs, frogs, clams, and snapping turtles. In the waters nearby were fresh whitefish, pickerel, eels, and nine-foot sturgeon. Little wonder that this Milwaukee country had long been a favorite gathering place for half a dozen native tribes.

When Kilbourn arrived on the scene, there was not much evidence of human habitation in the area – only a cluster of log structures belonging to Solomon Juneau and his brother Peter, and a small Indian village with its customary plantings of corn, squash, and beans. Acres of wild rice lined the bank of the river amid a forest of tamarack, cedar, ash, and black alder.[4] As Byron took in the scene before him, his mind focused not on natural beauty but on development and change. Milwaukee, he decided, would make a fine site for a city.

George Walker

Kilbourn remounted his horse and descended from the bluff to the riverbank. He tied his horse to a tree and crossed the river in a hollowed-out log. When Byron presented himself at the fur trader's door, Juneau was entertaining two important visitors: Judge Doty and Juneau's new partner from Green Bay, Morgan Martin. All three men greeted Kilbourn warmly as they would any stranger who came their way in this remote place. None had previously met the newcomer from Ohio, but they all knew of his famous employer, Micajah Williams, the surveyor general. It was Williams who determined what government land was to be put on sale and when. As one of Williams' agents, Kilbourn was clearly a person worth cultivating.

For over a dozen years, Solomon Juneau had been a seasonal resident in the Milwaukee area; his permanent home was 120 miles north in Green Bay. But in 1833, he moved his family to the east side of Milwaukee and, by so doing, became the city's first permanent resident. A genial host, Juneau was popular with whites and Native Americans alike. Byron later described him as "one of Nature's noblemen, a perfect gentleman."[5] Good-natured and easygoing, this French Canadian trader was the sort of man whose decisions were guided by his heart rather than his head. Although he came to acquire many thousands of dollars, he had no personal ambition, and was apparently unaware that the bayou before his door would soon become a busy waterway or that a populous town was about to be established at his doorstep.

The story goes that Juneau, in Milwaukee's early days, used to keep his cash in his tall hat. One day, the wind blew the hat off,

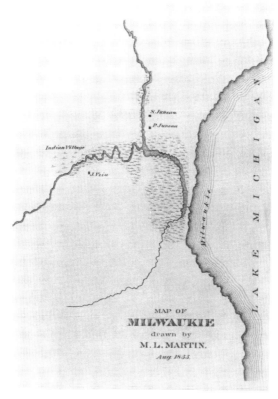

Morgan Martin's 1833
Map of Milwaukee.

34

and hundreds of dollars scattered on the street. Passersby scrambled for the bills while Juneau merely laughed and went on his way.

If vision was not a part of Juneau's makeup, it was in abundant supply among his three guests. Judge Doty, a long-time resident of the Michigan Territory, speculated in lands at Green Bay as well as in the Lake Winnebago region, and most notably at Four Lakes, the site of the future city of Madison. It was Doty who persuaded Wisconsin legislators to make Madison the capital of the territory, in the process providing deeds to choice in-town lots to sway reluctant lawmakers. When he met Kilbourn, Doty was not a key player at Milwaukee, but the following May he attempted to dominate the action by offering, on behalf of a New York conglomerate, to buy out Juneau and Martin in return for ten percent of the profits he made on the sale of their land – an offer quickly rejected. In time, Doty became Wisconsin's territorial delegate to Congress, and then territorial governor.[6]

Like Kilbourn, Morgan Martin visualized a future city at the mouth of the Milwaukee. Because his partner, Juneau, had been an early resident, territorial law allowed him to lay claim to property on both sides of the river. Martin instructed Juneau on how to protect their property from claim jumpers and recommended improvements to lure new settlers. Like Doty, he, too, was destined for political prominence and would one day chair the convention that produced Wisconsin's state constitution. Juneau and Martin decided to focus their attention upon the east side, a hilly wedge of land somewhat over a mile wide between river and lake. This left the land west of the river, with its unobstructed access to the interior, open for Kilbourn and Williams.

At first, all four developers cooperated with one another. Williams arranged to have the Milwaukee lands in which all four were interested included in a forthcoming land sale at Green Bay. Timing was critical if they were to beat rival speculators. Kilbourn joined Martin in land speculation at Green Bay and Kaukauna. And the four partners exchanged parcels of land on either side of the Milwaukee River to round out their spread. Five months after their initial meeting, Juneau and Martin offered to merge their interests with Kilbourn and Williams so they could develop the entire region together,[7] but this proposition was rejected by the partners from Ohio, thus laying the groundwork for competition rather than cooperation in Milwaukee's early years. The three sections of the future city – east, west and south – would vie with one another for settlers and leadership.

Morgan Martin reported that he, Doty, and Kilbourn "spent a few days being entertained" at Juneau's "hospitable old trading house, the only habitation there."[8] No record exists of what the four said to one another as they contemplated the future of Milwaukee, but we know that Kilbourn emerged from the meeting convinced that no one stood in his way as he and Williams planned their town on the west bank of the Milwaukee River. In the years that followed, Byron and the two shrewd New York lawyers, Doty and Martin, crossed paths frequently, more often than not as rivals in the development of frontier Wisconsin.

May 5, 1835, Kilbourn and Williams signed a formal partnership. They agreed to put up $8,000 for the purchase of land at the Green Bay sale, scheduled for midsummer. The usual practice in purchasing government land was to put ten percent down, and pay the remainder in equal installments in three to five years.

Partnership funds could thus extend much further than one might expect. If land prices rose rapidly, as every speculator was sure they would, buyers would have no difficulty in meeting their mortgage payments. If prices remained the same, or declined, they would be over extended and lose their property; hence, the element of risk. Land speculation was a perfectly respectable profession in a frontier community; everyone who could afford to engaged in the practice.

The Kilbourn-Williams contract called for Byron to be the partner on the scene. He was authorized to select the lands for purchase. He chose parcels north of the Menominee River and west of the Milwaukee River, plus additional property Martin hoped to develop on the Fox River at Kaukauna and on the East River in Green Bay.

Earlier, as a canal engineer in Ohio, Byron had saved his money; he had purchased a farm on the Muskingham River and several lots at Sandusky and Lockbourne, towns his father and brother laid out. He still had the money he received from the sale of these properties to buy land. In addition, he had $8,500 from others to invest, on the condition that he receive one half of whatever profits were made.[9]

Returning to Ohio, Kilbourn prepared for the upcoming sale with his customary thoroughness. Concerned about traveling alone, through hundreds of miles of wilderness with a large sum of money, he invited Garrett Vliet, his newly hired surveyor from Cincinnati, to travel with him. His anxiety to return to the west is reflected in a letter he wrote May 23, 1835 to Williams: "The sooner I can get to Green Bay to make deals the better. The sooner the better is the proper maxim in this case as perhaps in most cases of business." In mid-June, Kilbourn delivered a package for Williams to the registrar of the land office in Chicago. Sending valuable documents by private courier was often a safer and faster means of transport in those days than the irregular mail service.

From late June to mid-October, Byron resided at the village of Navarino at Green Bay. He anticipated fraud by those anxious "to establish preemptions and floats," but he did not think they would be sustained. On August 18, he assured Williams that arrangements could be made with other speculators on the scene to limit competitive bidding, "if not interrupted by the arrival of crazy fools from Chicago." Limiting competition was deemed an acceptable practice in an era when business ethics were ill-defined. "I have been detained here much longer than I expected to complete arrangements wch [sic] consumes much time," Byron wrote. But it was time well spent. "I've had 30-40 applications for lots ... all we need to go ahead is to get the plat [Vliet's survey map] run off and authority to sell [from the General Land Office in Washington, D.C.]." Both obstacles would be overcome by early January, 1836.

Kilbourn also told Williams he thought he could get better rates for Milwaukee lots by selling them in Chicago, for "Milwaukee is in high repute" there. While "the tide is flowing," and before Juneautown, east of the river, got too great a start, "is the time to strike." (Juneau had already erected fifteen buildings on the east side.) On October 6, Byron reported that he sold Alexander Clybourn of Chicago a sixteenth interest in the Kilbourn-Williams speculation for $5,000; another sixteenth went to "Mr. Rogers" of New York, and a further share to Colonel McCarty of Virginia. Clybourn seconded Kilbourn's scheme to sell Milwaukee lots in Chicago and suggested appropriate advertising. "I have but little doubt," Byron noted on October 16, "that within two years Milwaukee will produce a very handsome fund." Given the opportunity to make his fortune, Byron left nothing to chance. He sold fifty-six lots on credit before leaving Milwaukee for Chicago. His purpose was twofold: to create the illusion of a brisk market and to interest Chicagoans in land west of the river.

The Green Bay land sale took place between July 30 and August 9, 1835. The preceding June, Congress had revived the federal preemption law of 1830. This statute stipulated that squatters on government lands who erected "a building" and began "improvements" should be given first right of purchase at the time their spread came on the market. Since neither Kilbourn nor Williams fit this description their names do not appear on the rolls as original proprietors. What does appear, on August 1, 3, and 5, are the entries of John B. Genor, Peter Chilifon, Joseph Jourdain, and Lewis Rouse, men who possessed "floating rights" to Milwaukee land. Once their proprietorship was established, they sold their newly acquired land to Byron Kilbourn. In this way, he and Williams secured title to 281.47 acres of prime Milwaukee land for $351.84, at the going rate of $1.25 per acre. The new community Byron founded west of the river came to be known as Kilbourntown.[10]

Once his claims were registered at the nation's capital, Byron sent the following triumphant letter to his father in Ohio:

> Until now my business has been in so unsettled a
> condition that I did not wish to speak of it in

relation to value which I anticipated from my N. Western speculation – I thought it better to beat the bush carefully until I caught the bird – I now have it safely caged – my patents are issued and in my possession – I will now say to you that my interests at the N.W. are worth $100,000 without over estimating them one farthing. My share in the Sales already made are rising of $20,000, about $8000 of which I have received in cash – enabling me to discharge my bank loan of $6000 – defray all other expenses, and leave a small residue – I have no doubt of realizing a larger Sum than that stated if times remain as they have been, but that Sum I consider a Safe estimate with any State of affairs which we have any reason to look for – [11]

Like James Kilbourne before him, Byron made no mention of having financial partners. It was Micajah Williams, after all, who had lent him the $6,000 that made a major portion of this speculation possible. Note also the cautious tone of this letter; Byron is unwilling to announce his good news until his patents are signed, sealed, and delivered.

The $100,000 estimate Kilbourn cites represented potential market value, not cash in hand. In fact, this figure proved conservative. In October of 1836, less than nine months later, Increase Lapham, Byron's business agent, told his Ohio relatives that "the amount of sales of town lots by Kilbourn and Williams is now about $220,000," their initial investment having been a mere $3,000. [12]

To grasp the significance of Byron's coup, we need to keep in mind that a farm laborer in the 1830s earned between $96 and $120 a year, and that eastern industrial workers earned between $60 and $300 for the same period. Thirty thousand dollars was considered a "fortune." Yet Byron accumulated real estate profits over *three times* this amount in twelve months! In effect, he became a wealthy man overnight – at least on paper. As if to advertise his sudden affluence, Kilbourn ordered the construction of Milwaukee's first brick house. His father, James, had done precisely the same thing at Worthington in 1804.

The Kilbourn-Williams correspondence of 1835-37 provides us with a clear picture of the business activities of the two partners.[13] As the local agent, Byron was viewed as the "active partner." He set up a real estate office and led all others in developing the new community west of the river. Meanwhile, Williams attended to his widespread affairs from his business office in Cincinnati. Like Morgan Martin, he provided practical advice and secured cash for investment.

Both partners were interested in attracting new money to help defray the cost of needed improvements, but they fully intended to remain in charge. They were willing to enter into collaboration with a Clybourn or the McCarty brothers of Virginia, and Byron persuaded well-to-do Ohioans, such as the Comstocks of Worthington, and Joel Buttles and Dr. I. G. Jones of Columbus, to provide financial backing. But the key decisions remained in the hands of the two original partners.

Initially, Byron used his own money in land speculation, but Williams suggested that he shift from personal investment to serving as agent for absentee landowners. Eastern men with money provided him with their powers of attorney and the where-withal to buy choice lots as these came on the market. (Morgan Martin and James Doty operated in much the same way.) In return for his services, Kilbourn received a share of the profits. He was also empowered to trade lots among owners as he saw fit. Throughout Wisconsin's territorial period (1836-48), Byron was land poor and continually in debt. He was a master at juggling one account against another, but sometimes he had to ask Williams to bail him out when income fell short of expectation.

In 1836 everything seemed to be going Byron's way. His gamble on Milwaukee real estate paid off handsomely. As Mary happily wrote her stepsister, "I have the pleasure to inform you that Mr. Kilbourn has succeeded in establishing all his floats except one, and in entering all his lots but one that he wished; he says that he has thereby laid a cornerstone for a fortune of twenty to thirty thousand dollars, which cannot he thinks well fail him." Two months later, in November of 1835, Mary told her Connecticut relatives that "many New York speculators have tried this summer pretty hard to get hold of the best part of Milwaukee, but Mr. K. has outwitted them, as well as some of the residents of the Territory."[14] Clearly Mary was proud of her husband's accomplishments.

This was the year Mary and the children came to join Byron in Milwaukee. After months of planning, the family arrived in July. Byron drove a two-horse wagon equipped with a bed on which Mary could recline whenever she grew tired of sitting up. Except for her state of health, the family's future looked bright. Dr. Jones, Cynthia Kilbourn's husband, had restored her "to such a degree of health and strength" that she was unwilling to remain longer in Ohio "when her husband must be mainly in Wisconsin."[15]

When Mary and Byron were showing friends about the site of their new home, Mary developed a chill which became persistent. Soon she was out of medicine, and had no way of procuring more. "Little more could be done, than to wait patiently until the [shipping] season came round" when she could return to Worthington for medical care. It was mid-June before the first steamer arrived. On April 10, with unsteady hand and painful effort, she wrote a final letter to her parents. She died en route to Worthington on June 24.[16]

Land fever swept the upper Midwest. Increase Lapham, hired as Byron Kilbourn's business agent, described the scene thus, "I am now & have been since I arrived at Sandusky in what may properly be called the World of Speculators – every body you meet is engaged in some speculation – every thing you hear has some speculation at the bottom. The hotel where I am now writing has suspended on the walls of the Bar Room 8 plats of new towns & I have added the 9th!"[17] In 1836, Milwaukee became a speculator's paradise, the "Las Vegas" of the Wisconsin Territory. As reported by the area's first newspaper, the *Green Bay Intelligencer*, "land speculators are circumambuling it and Milwauky is all the rage."

Byron Kilbourn was a risk taker. He lived constantly on the edge, but with great expectations based on land and investments. His efforts on behalf of road construction, an improved harbor, a canal, and railroads were all motivated by his desire for profit, to be sure, but these projects also enhanced the public welfare. Like large landowners elsewhere, he could not always lay his hands on ready cash, but he was affluent enough to survive the economic panic of 1837. As a reporter noted when he ran for territorial representative to Congress two years later, Kilbourn *campaigned in a carriage.* He purchased butter in the bitter winter of 1838 at *twice the normal price,* and his handsome brick home at Chestnut and Third became a local landmark.[18]

In addition to serving as agent for eastern investors, Kilbourn often lent money to incoming settlers. If the newcomers prospered, he collected his principal and short-term interest and bought more land elsewhere. If the borrower came upon hard times and was unable to discharge his debt, Byron repossessed the property with whatever improvements had been made and sold it again at a higher price. Either way he stood to gain. In a frontier community where cash was scarce, he was in an excellent position to take advantage of real estate opportunities.

Buying and selling Milwaukee property became Byron's key to wealth. In contrast to Morgan Martin, whose investments were widespread, Kilbourn made Milwaukee his base. The gradual availability of money for investment in the 1840s and '50s, the development of local water power made possible by the canal he championed, and the fortuitous migration of a steady flow of hard-working German immigrants to provide a labor force all combined to ensure Milwaukee's prosperity in the antebellum era.

Three themes dominated the next quarter century of

Kilbourn's life: urban development, transportation, and finance. The lots Byron had to sell increased in value as local improvements made them more attractive. The first step in this process involved filling in the wetlands along the Milwaukee River. No one could expect buyers to purchase property that was under water much of the year. Gravel fill came from the bluffs to the west, and silt was dredged from the Milwaukee River.

New settlers also needed a place where they could buy groceries and other essentials. They needed roads, sidewalks, and a school for their children. They needed a local person familiar with the area, someone who could advise them on what property to purchase. In all these matters Byron Kilbourn played a role. And more. Kilbourn became the community's preeminent promoter, advertising Milwaukee's virtues far and wide. His motive was simple: as Milwaukee grew, so, too, did the profits from the land he had to sell.

Because Kilbourntown did not border Lake Michigan, ready access from the bay of Milwaukee and from Chicago to the south was critical. Therefore, Byron focused his efforts on transportation: first on roads and packet boats, later on a canal to connect Milwaukee with the Mississippi, and finally on railroads. For over a quarter century he championed harbor improvement. Indeed, no project for Milwaukee's development escaped his attention: as two local historians put it, "Kilbourn was a key figure in nearly every significant public and private venture affecting Milwaukee as well as the state."[19]

Having capital to invest is a major necessity for any developer. Kilbourn was no different from the rest. He could count on the aid of Micajah Williams and friends and relatives in Ohio, and he could manage funds for eastern capitalists. But in the matter of large internal improvements, he was dependent upon government – territorial, federal, state, and municipal. His task was to persuade public officials that the projects he favored were in the best interests of the people at large, and therefore deserved to be funded. To a remarkable degree, he was successful, swaying congressmen to support the territory's first land grant, securing state charters for new railroads, and getting the Milwaukee Common Council to invest heavily in his railroads. Not all the projects he envisioned were funded, but a surprising number were. More than any other man, more than Solomon Juneau or George Walker, Kilbourn led the way in the early days of Milwaukee's development.

On January 29, 1836, Kilbourn wrote a persuasive letter to Missouri Senator Lewis Linn, half brother of Territorial Governor Henry Dodge, seeking his support for harbor improvement. Linn was a leading advocate of internal improvements for the rapidly developing west, so it was appropriate that Byron contact him. His plea for federal funds for harbor improvement, a project critical to Milwaukee's future, merits our attention: "The Milwaukee [River] is decidedly the largest stream which discharges into Lake Michigan on its western coast and affords facilities for the construction of a harbor not possessed by any other stream on that side of the lake. There are other streams which may, and doubtless will, be improved for harbors ere long, but it is presumed that the Government will, in the first instance, select such points for early improvement, as unite the greatest advantages, both in regard to the feasibility of construction and position, for the transactions of commercial business."

In surveyor-like fashion Byron went on to describe the locale: "By reference to a map of this region, as derived from the actual surveys, it will be seen that this river reaches the lake at its greatest western bend, at which point there is a deep indentation of the shore, forming a spacious bay, into which the river has its discharge. The bay will form a safe and easy entrance into the harbor when constructed.... The bar at the mouth of the river is narrow," Kilbourn admitted. "Indeed it is peculiar in this respect and different from most of the rivers on the lakes, there being but a small amount of drifting sand which may accumulate by any agitation of the water, or direction of the wind." The water in the river itself "is very deep, and the shores bold, and outside of the bar, the lake deepens within a distance of six or eight rods to ten or twelve feet water, and thence goes off with a bold descent, and clay bottom, having no tendency to wash, drift, or change its position, thus leaving free forever any channel which may be made.... The river is of such volume," he added, "that it would immediately produce its own channel, if protected in the manner of harbors on Lake Erie, and the extent of works required, would be far less than any harbor with which I am acquainted on that Lake. It is my impression that the piers would not exceed one hundred yards in length" while those at Cleveland and elsewhere "are about a quarter of a mile, and the cost of these piers would probably be reduced in the same ratio."

Turning to the question of harbor construction, Kilbourn observed that "all the materials for the work may be obtained within a short distance of the point of operation." A stone quarry was only three miles away, and timber was readily available "either up the river, or along the lake, and delivered at the cheapest possible rate by water."[20]

Byron Kilbourn was not the first to urge the government to act; eighty-four "owners and masters of Great Lakes Vessels" had requested $15,000 for Milwaukee harbor improvement more than a year earlier. But he was a persistent advocate of this cause for twenty-one years before the "straight cut" he favored – a direct entrance into the upper Milwaukee River harbor – was finally built.

On March 1, 1836, Kilbourn announced the opening of his real estate office.[21] Meanwhile, in Washington, Congress considered four Milwaukee-related bills: a petition for $50,000 to open a road to the west, a bill to establish a lighthouse, the establishment of a new government land office, and an appropriation to improve the harbor. The second and third of these proposals became law soon after.

Returning to Ohio, Byron recruited workers for his new town, and in mid-April, he invited Increase Lapham, his former rod man on the Miami Canal, to come west and become his business agent. Kilbourn offered Lapham the choice of a salary of $800 per year or a quarter of the profits to be derived from his new land agency. He also asked Micajah Williams to advance travel funds for Lapham's trip west.

Kilbourn established his real estate office beside his house and installed Lapham there to oversee his business transactions during his frequent absences from the city. Lapham was ten years younger than Byron. The son of a New York canal contractor, he had become Byron's assistant on the Miami Canal at age fifteen. A lifelong student of geology and mineralogy, "not from books but from observation," Lapham possessed an insatiable curiosity about the world around him. At sixteen, he published his first scientific paper with the Smithsonian Institution, and many others followed. At Milwaukee, he embarked on a distinguished career in geography, cartography, archeology, botany, zoology, and meteorology. In 1844, he published a geography of the territory,

Increase Lapham

the first substantive book to appear in Wisconsin history. So extensive, diverse, and systematic were his investigations that Lapham became known as Wisconsin's first great scientist.[22]

Increase Lapham was far more than a collector of curiosities, as his published studies and extensive correspondence with scientists throughout the world prove. Earlier, in 1833, he had been appointed to the responsible position of secretary of the Ohio Board of Canal Commissioners, a post he ably filled for three years, when he was replaced by a political appointee. In time, Lapham became Byron's confidant and best friend. When Kilbourn drew up his will in 1868, he made Lapham co-executor, along with his own son Byron Hector.[23] Lapham was loyal, efficient, and dependable, a man of unquestioned integrity. Byron could not have made a wiser choice.

On April 16, Byron asked Williams what he thought of "building a tavern house" in their new town. We do not know Williams' response, but we do know that Byron became a major backer of "Leland's Pavilion," where the Milwaukee County Historical Society now stands.[24] By any standard of measurement, 1836 was a critical year in Milwaukee development.

A group of New York speculators contemplated establishing a regular source of water power at a dam on the Milwaukee River, a short distance north of Kilbourn's house. But on June 17th, Lapham informed Williams that Byron had secured these rights "at a great speculation."[25] Kilbourn and Williams were not in favor of every internal improvement, however. They opposed the construction of a bridge over the Milwaukee River. Their argument was that such a structure would impede free navigation on the river, a right guaranteed by the Northwest Ordinance of 1787. But their real purpose was to isolate the east side. Should Williams lose his suit to block construction, Kilbourn declared he could use steam-boats to keep the bridge permanently open, thereby disrupting pedestrian traffic.[26] The partners' strategy was clear: isolate Juneau's east side to ensure that newcomers would come to the west side when they wanted to buy property.

Every coastal town from Kewaunee to Kenosha was Milwaukee's competitor. Both Sheboygan and Port Washington had better natural harbors, and their supporters were so vociferous at the time some Milwaukeeans actually pulled up stakes and moved farther north. On December 5, 1836, Kilbourn told Williams that the army engineers who surveyed the Milwaukee harbor had been ordered to return to their companies before reporting their findings. A congressional appropriation that winter was accordingly unlikely. To move the work forward, Byron reported, the citizens of Kilbourntown "have determined to raise a subscription of $25,000 and commence the work. This sum will open a channel and extend the piers a sufficient distance to protect it, whereby we will be able to admit vessels next season, and give stimulus to business. The amt. will be refunded when our appropriation is made; and the measure seems not only to be necessary but will I have no doubt enhance the value of property much beyond cost."[27] Despite the desirability of the project, securing $25,000 in the Wisconsin Territory in 1836 was impossible. The improvement would have to wait for another day.

Byron's interest in internal improvements was unquestionably based on self-interest. He and his fellow speculators hoped to increase the value of their holdings by providing better means of access. Rapid development was essential if Milwaukee were to prosper, for there were many fledgling communities aspiring to greatness in the Great Lakes region. No one knew this better than he, and so he now engaged in a flurry of activity that must have astounded his peers. Months before the patent to his land was secure, Byron hired local workmen to begin filling in the tamarack swamp. They were also to construct a bridge over the Menominee River so that traffic headed north on the Chicago road would come directly to Kilbourntown rather than taking passage on Juneau's ferry to the east side.[28] This Menominee bridge also drew traffic away from George Walker's development on the south side.

On one of his trips back east, Kilbourn hired Garret Vliet of

Cincinnati to lay out his township west of the river. Vliet completed this task four months before Kilbourn and Williams secured final title to their land. Vliet followed the checkerboard pattern commonly used in the Northwest Territory. While this gridiron system resulted in "a large number of uniform lots," it made no allowance for topographical irregularities, such as a bend in the Milwaukee River. Vliet's survey produced 510 buildable lots, plus the land for two public squares.[29] The original Kilbourn-Williams purchase at Milwaukee included all the land located between Juneau Avenue on the north and the Menominee River on the south, and between 6th Street on the west and the Milwaukee River on the east. (Byron later acquired much additional property in the area.)

Across the river, Juneautown was being platted at about the same time. To emphasize the fact that the two communities were separate from one another, Kilbourn directed that the roads on his side of the river be laid out so they would not line up with Juneau's, a peculiarity apparent to this day.

It is one thing to lay out a town on paper, but quite another to prepare lots for sale. Many newcomers thought the bluff on the west side of Kilbourn's purchase too steep for building sites. And they were equally deterred by the swampy area bordering the river itself. One advocate of this point of view conveyed his sentiments in a letter he wrote to his sister, August 3, 1835:

> Well, here I am with your Joseph, but never have I seen a more God-damned place in my life. The town – or what is so called – lies in the middle of a swamp. One cannot go one half mile in any direction without getting into water. The entire place is a deep morass. The river is a very fine thing – as I expected – but when you have to cross it 3 or 4 times daily on a log it ceases to be an enjoyment. Joseph has built his house far on the other side of the river where the wolves jump over his fence, but where the town will never reach him.

[Joseph's house stood in the neighborhood of 9th Street.] But what good will it do for me to continue writing. He has completely fallen in love with the place and wants you to come here. If, however, I had my way, you should remain in our old Detroit. I often wish I were there again.

In similar fashion, Harry Cleveland's brother asked him "what he was going to do with such a God-forsaken piece of hill and slough" as his claim on the west side. "Build a city on it," Harry replied. "I'll level down the hills to fill up the sloughs," and it will make "a fine location for a city." Whereupon his brother laughed him to scorn.[30] The skeptics notwithstanding, Cleveland's remedy was precisely the solution Byron Kilbourn had in mind. An experienced canal engineer, he knew how to level a landscape.

Long before earth-moving equipment was available, an enormous amount of manual labor was needed to prepare the site. Pioneer historian James Buck explained:

> All that portion of the Fourth Ward bounded by the Menominee on the south, the Milwaukee on the east, Spring Street [the present Wisconsin Avenue] on the north, and to a point about midway between Fourth and Fifth Streets on the west, where the hill commenced, was a wild rice swamp, covered with water two to six feet in depth, in fact, an impassable marsh. The amount of filling that has been done on this portion is immense, *averaging twenty-two feet on the entire tract.* At Spring Street the ground commenced to harden, and from there to Chestnut [now Juneau Avenue] . . . the whole was a swamp upon which grew tamarack, black ash, tag alder, and cedar in abundance. . . . At Chestnut Street the ground was hard enough to build upon, and it was here that Kilbourn commenced his city.

Once the swamp was drained, fill was needed, and the nearby gravel bluff was cut *"from ten to forty feet* in order to make the streets, running west and north, practicable." Buck added that *"sixty to seventy feet of fill* was necessary in some places to bring Spring Street up to grade" [emphasis added]. Captain William Donahoe, another eyewitness to these labor-intensive improvements, noted that "the Milwaukee River was dredged and dirt dumped along the dock, and when dry enough, was leveled and helped to make a road along on either side of the river."[31] The *Milwaukee Advertiser* of September 1836, reported that Kilbourn and Juneau together "employ about 150 men at present, grading and improving the streets they have laid out. They are spending $40,000 for the purpose this year." So widespread was the need for internal improvement that every male resident between twenty-one and sixty was "required to work two days per week on the roads, streets and alleys or pay two dollars." Street grading and sidewalk construction continued for a decade after Kilbourntown was founded.[32]

Byron Kilbourn played a major role in every activity that affected his new town. He was an early road commissioner, and as president of the town he let contracts for road construction and grading. Thoroughfares known as "Kilbourn roads" extended south at 11th Street to the old Mukwonago Road at the present Forest Home Cemetery, as well as west to Waukesha.[33] But surface transportation would count for little if Kilbourntown remained an isolated, inland community. Water access was crucial if the town were to attract new settlers and grow. Roads throughout the Midwest at the time were poorly maintained and often impassable for several months of the year. Transportation by water was the key to settlement, and would remain so for many years to come.

Barring a northeast gale, passenger ships in Lake Michigan had no trouble anchoring in the Bay of Milwaukee, but there was no way they could enter the Milwaukee River, for the depth of the water at the bar was barely six feet. Kilbourn's immediate need, therefore, was for a shallow-draft vessel that could meet passing ships and ferry passengers and freight through the inner harbor to his west side dock. In the spring of 1837, he hired Captain Samuel Hubbell to create such a craft for him. The result was the fifty-ton steamer, *Badger*, a lighter 64 feet in length, 12 feet in beam, which drew a mere two feet of water. The *Badger* was powered by a twenty horsepower engine. Her cabin could hold as many as one hundred passengers in inclement weather, and the experienced Captain Hubbell could use her to tow schooners in and out of the bay when wind power was insufficient.

The *Badger* ran from Kilbourn's dock at the foot of Chestnut Street to the bay and back, stopping at Chase's point on the south side each hour. Under the owner's strict orders, the captain made no stops at Juneau's east side. If passengers wished to travel to Juneautown, they had to land first at Kilbourn's dock on the west side, then walk five blocks south to catch Matthew Keenan's ferry. "Passengers were told that Kilbourntown was the city proper, and that Juneautown was little more than an Indian trading post."

The July 4, 1837, *Milwaukee Sentinel* described the *Badger's* maiden voyage in its best booster fashion:

> Our waters were enlivened last Saturday by the appearance of a new and elegant scow – the '*Badger.*' She was built, and is owned, we are informed, by that enterprising citizen, Mr. Byron Kilbourn.... For several days previous public expectation as been on the *qui vive* awaiting her first appearance on any waters. And here at length she did appear, we need not add that the expectations of her most sanguine admirers were fully realized. Early in the morning smoke was seen by those on the 'lookout' to ascend from the polished chimneys of the *Badger* and soon it was spread about that she was expecting the arrival of the Bunkerhill and would pay her a complimentary visit to greet her on her arrival in the harbor. But unfortunately the expected visitant did not arrive and it was determined that the Badger should make

a pleasure excursion over her future course to the mouth of the river. At the appointed time, heaving in the water, and impatient of restraint, she started beautifully from her moorings and as she passed Milwaukee we had a fine view of her noble proportions and splendid finish. With her deep toned engine under full power, and with all her streamers flying, she presented to the eye of taste the gratifying spectacle of beauty, power, and speed combined in one graceful fabric majestically moving through the deep water of our beautiful river, and 'going it with the most perfect looseness.' We understand she was something less than an hour in making her trip to the mouth of the river (stoppage excepted). The party returned highly delighted with the excursion and though the 'Heavers were hung in black' we doubt not if the sun had been out in Heaven, his parting ray would have lingered on the beautiful summit of the Badgers chimney.[34]

One early historian noted that the *Badger* "was capable of alarming the entire town when it arrived by its truly diabolical whistling, snorting, and splashing as it stirred the calm river into wild waves, and flooded the banks." The voyage from the bay to Kilbourn's dock was safe and fast, so long as "the wheels did not get too deeply entangled in the wild rice and weeds." The charge for passengers was twenty-five to fifty cents. While Kilbourn's west siders were proud of their little steamer, Juneau's east siders regarded it with scorn. Every time the *Badger* "puffed its way up the Milwaukee River, it cut into the tender feelings of the people of Juneautown, because, belonging to Byron Kilbourn, it was not permitted to land on the east side."[35]

Taking advantage of the ready availability of local lumber and skilled labor, Kilbourn ordered the construction of three more steam vessels in 1837: the 55-ton *Savannah*, the 70-ton *Bolivar*, and the 75-ton *Menominee*. The *Savannah* and the *Menominee*

*Mural of Byron Kilbourn overseeing
the construction of a new boat.*

joined the *Badger* in hauling passengers to and from visiting ships in the bay.

Kilbourn became involved in another maritime project, part ownership of the lake steamer *Detroit*. A double-decker vessel of 137 tons, the *Detroit* was 125 feet long and had a beam of 17 feet 6 inches. Constructed in 1833 at Swan Creek, Michigan, her home port was Michigan City, Indiana. Her schedule was designed to connect with a series of daily stages arriving from Toledo and Detroit. She made trips three times weekly from Michigan City to Milwaukee, passing the bar at the mouth of the river with ease. The *Detroit* was the first steam packet to travel to Milwaukee on a regular schedule, although regular steamboat service had existed between Buffalo and Chicago since 1834. This promising venture proved to be short-lived, however; the economic depression of 1837 ended the *Detroit's* visits after a single season.[36]

Even though shifting sands and shallow depths impeded Milwaukee's development as a port in the early years, the growth of ship traffic was still impressive. While only two steamships visited the harbor in 1835, four years later there were 182. Sailing vessels numbered 80 at the earlier date, but mushroomed to 290 two years later. City imports amounted to $590,000 in a one-year period from 1835 to 1836, rising to $1,800,000 five years later.[37]

Despite such growth, every Milwaukeean believed the city's commercial potential was far greater. Visiting vessels were required to anchor out in the bay and depend upon tenders to take goods and passengers to shore. If only the federal government would provide the funds necessary for dredging and piers, a large, protected inner harbor would become available. But President Andrew Jackson did not believe that funding internal improvements was constitutional. When the government in Washington finally did act, its appropriation was much too small to do the job.

Exasperated by the slowness with which government worked, Byron Kilbourn decided to take matters into his own hands. One night in June 1843, he sent a crew of a hundred of his men to a point half a mile north of the river's mouth. There they dug a passage through to the Milwaukee River. However, a permanent opening required greater effort than this. On June 17, the citizens of Kilbourntown voted to borrow money to build piers at the cut. But the funds could not be raised.

The "straight cut" proposal became a political issue in the election of 1839. As a candidate for territorial delegate to Congress, Kilbourn favored the plan while James Doty, his principal opponent, opposed it. Doty won the election and "here the matter rested for a great while." Harbor improvement became a major plank in Kilbourn's political platform when he ran for mayor in

1848, but the job was not actually completed until 1857. Kilbourn's "straight cut" remains in use to the present day.

Byron not only urged federal authorities to improve the harbor but also took matters into his own hands when he thought funds were being squandered at the river's mouth, and in general did all in his power to advance harbor improvement. His will was strong but funds were scarce – a condition all too common in Wisconsin's territorial period.

At the junction of Chestnut and Third beside the river, Byron erected a house, office, store, dock, and warehouse. No business opportunity escaped his attention. What incoming settlers to Milwaukee most needed was reliable information to help them in

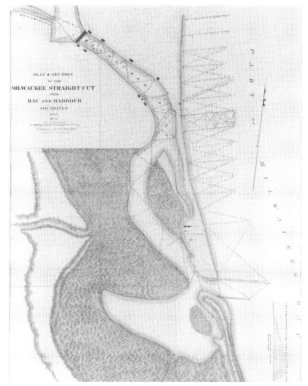

The Milwaukee Harbor "Straight Cut"
long advocated by Byron Kilbourn and
finally completed in 1857.

56

the purchase of land. They sought a person familiar with the local scene upon whose judgment they could depend. Byron Kilbourn presented himself as just such a person. In ads placed in key newspapers in New York City, Albany, Buffalo, and Detroit, as well as in Milwaukee, he emphasized his background as a territorial surveyor familiar with the area's natural resources, and his willingness to serve as agent for those who wished to sell property purchased earlier. "To advance the objects of this agency," Byron said, "a registry will be kept of all sales made, at the several land offices in the territory...." Prospective buyers could count on receiving only the most up-to-date information. Government surveyors are the most knowledgeable land experts one can find in any new territory. As one of these, Kilbourn clearly had an edge over his rivals. His ads were skillfully designed to appeal to *both* the settler and the speculator. Further, since most new arrivals came west by way of the Erie Canal, his ads were strategically placed. When he sold his agency to Lapham three years later, only 100 of the original 510 lots on the west side remained on the market.[38]

In addition to his flourishing real estate business, Byron became involved in a venture of a quite different sort: he subsidized the establishment of a general store. The firm was called S. D. Cowles & Co. and was managed by Sylvester Dering Cowles, his wife's stepbrother. Born in Connecticut in 1808, "Dering" was attracted to new business opportunities in the west. On November 30, 1835, Mary wrote her parents that her husband "wishes Dering to go" into business with him. Byron contracted for the building of a house and store, to be completed the following April. "If you have not written Dering on the subject, I wish you would do so in order that he may be weighing the pros and cons...." Byron had no doubt it would be in Dering's best interest to join him in Milwaukee. "I think it will be an excellent chance for him," Mary added. "Mr. K. says he is not at all disappointed in his anticipations of Milwaukee, except that property is likely to run to a higher valuation sooner than expected.... I hope our parents," she told her brother, Rensselaer, "will be in favor of Dering's going with Mr. Kilbourn as I think he will have much more of a prospect of doing well for himself with us, than in Conn."

Five months later, Mary again wrote her parents: "It is not probable Mr. K. would be able to go into any merchandising concern himself at present, as his plans are to invest what little funds he can raise in land speculation." The Kilbourn-Cowles partnership did eventually occur, as evidenced by the company's advertisement of its wares in Byron's newspaper, the *Milwaukee Advertiser*. The firm's stock included "ready made clothing": hats, boots and shoes, dry goods, hardware, glassware and cutlery, groceries, and school books – all "recently purchased in the eastern Cities with particular reference to the western market."

In the following months the store added lumber, ploughs, window glass, pork, ham and lard on consignment, cheese, butter, whiskey, eggs, green apples, seed wheat, carpet, and rugs. And a year later, S.D. Cowles & Co. was listed as passenger and freight agent for the steamship *Detroit*. Still later, the company advertised 2,000 cords of wood for sale – fuel no longer needed by the *Detroit* – plus "a large fishing net and boat." A commission warehouse was erected for the convenience of "immigrants and settlers." But to no avail. The partnership was dissolved two years, two months, and five days after it began, a casualty of the depression of 1837.[39]

As new settlers poured into Milwaukee, other phases of community development evolved. The first public school in the area was established on the west side in 1836, "Byron Kilbourn being one of its officers," and the firm of Kilbourn and Cowles supplied the textbooks. Hoping to secure the prize of a county courthouse, Kilbourn offered a free building lot for that purpose, but Juneau and Martin won the prize.[40]

As strange as it may seem today, "metropolitan" Milwaukee developed the first county agricultural society in the Wisconsin Territory. Although Kilbourn and Williams originally made a fortune in the sale of town lots, they had properties in the outlying areas as well, so to attract new buyers, Byron interested himself in the plight of the farmer. Ever the promoter, he arranged in December of 1836 for an exhibit of local products, "to convince the world of the superiority of Milwaukee," as he grandly put it. The success of this venture induced him to issue a call for the formation of a county agricultural society. Not surprisingly, Kilbourn was asked to preside, with Solomon Juneau serving as vice president, and the ever-resourceful Lapham, as secretary. Speaking to a settlers' group forty years later, Lapham recounted what happened next. The society's board of managers authorized the establishment of an experimental farm for the growth of livestock, "grain, fruit trees, and seeds." A county fair was scheduled for the following fall, at which prizes were given for the area's best produce. And articles describing sound agricultural practices were published in Kilbourn's newspaper. Though the history of the Milwaukee agricultural society was brief, Lapham believed its programs "had much influence in promoting the interests" of the local farmer.

Opening a store, starting an elementary school, organizing an agricultural society – these are all important signs of community development, but what most concerned outlying settlers was the security of their land. The federal preemption law had recently lapsed, and many farmers feared they would lose their land because they would no longer be allowed the first right of purchase, and in 1837 "encroachments were made upon what was deemed to be the rights" of first settlers, and a resort to force seemed likely. It was at this point that Kilbourn intervened and drafted a "code of laws" to resolve the dilemma. Under his arrangement, settlers proceeded to develop their claims without fear until, in due time, they were allowed to purchase their land at the standard government price of $1.25 an acre. Instead of the violence we associate with frontier justice, a peaceful solution prevailed.

On February 27, 1837, Kilbourn wrote Micajah Williams a full account of where their partnership stood. He reported that he bought out Alexander Clybourn "10 or 12 days since.... I have now made out a statement of receipts and expenditures up to Dec. 31, 1836 which shows a balance due you of $9875,70. I have nearly this sum in hand and propose to use it for the present in payment for work now progressing, but to be refunded out of future receipts.... My portion of the receipts has been entirely consumed, and a little more, in buildings & c., in addition to my part of road and street expenditures. My buildings alone have cost rising of $13,000, having been done under the most disadvantageous of circumstances." Kilbourn explained that "in Ohio, the same work could have been done for less than $5000. But it was important, in the highest degree, that the proprietors should do something in the way of improvement and business, by way of giving an impulse, and to counterbalance in some degree the effects on the other side made by the proprietors there." Competition from across the river served as a constant spur to Kilbourn in Milwaukee's earliest days.

"The effect produced by taking the lead in improvement," Kilbourn continued, "may be seen by that around my residence. Although so far up the river, there is now a very respectable village around me," little of which would be here "but for the commencement made by me." Byron recommended that the partners construct one or two new buildings, "to give a connected appearance" to Kilbourntown. The "appearance" of progress and prosperity was foremost in his thinking, much as it would be to the developer of a modern suburb.

But the economy was depressed and the days of the partnership with Williams were numbered. In May of 1837, Kilbourn reported that land sales had declined sharply because of the reduction in credit mandated by the federal government. He hoped that bad times in the east would mean good times in the west. The steamship *Madison* had just landed 300 settlers on Milwaukee's beaches, but these new arrivals quickly headed for the interior. Their stay in town was temporary and their purchases strictly limited to necessities.

Credit was the key to land speculation. As long as the federal government accepted the notes of local and regional banks, there would be no shortage of borrowers. However, the inflated currency made fraud possible so President Andrew Jackson took action. On July 11, 1836, his administration issued a "specie circular" stipulating that as of August 15, nothing but coined gold or silver would be acceptable as payment for government land. Jackson's measure took effect almost at once. After the 15th, "wild buying and selling of government lands" came to an abrupt halt.[41] "Milwaukee's real estate market collapsed virtually overnight. The town population of 1,200 dropped to 500 within a year. Lots purchased at $500 to $1,000 were traded for a barrel of flour to ward off starvation. "Corner-lots, paper towns and quarter sections of unimproved land had swallowed up and absorbed all our money," Dr. Lucius Barber recalled. "The great financial question of the day was 'how to redeem our shirts from the washer woman?'"[42]

Milwaukee was hit hard. On May 7, 1837, Kilbourn informed Micajah Williams that collections had been slow, and that he might soon be forced to halt improvements entirely. Later in the same month, he recommended that the partners move "cautiously" until the storm passed. Ever the optimist, Byron was convinced that Milwaukee real estate would retain its value in the long run, but at the moment, his income was negligible. No new construction began in the current season, and Kilbourn refrained for a time from suits for non-payment, "which wld probably be bad policy anyway, except in 'extreme cases.'"[43] Byron hoped that new immigrants from the east would bring salvation, and that an increase in population and farm production would bring Milwaukee "to that state of golden magnificence which the fond prophecy of its inhabitants has marked out for its destiny."

But an early recovery was not forthcoming. "Our town," Increase Lapham wrote his brother, "is not improving as much this summer as last.... Money is scarce, provisions scarce and dear.... We feel the pressure of the times here in the woods, very little doing in the way of improvements. In fact, Milwaukee begins to be a dull place and will have to jog along at the rate of other towns."[44]

Some local boosters predicted an overnight return to prosperity, but Byron Kilbourn thought otherwise. Three years after the crash, he confided to a New York investor that Milwaukee had been slow to recover: "When here you must have considered our place very dull, as it really is and has been since the first revulsion in money matters. Our country was then too recently settled to afford any surplus for export, and having all to purchase, without anything to sell, relying only on immigration to preserve our circulating medium – we had necessarily to retrench in everything until the products of our own country could bring us out. – This we shall in some measure realize this season, and still more so in the next, and we have no fears but business in every branch will revive. Our natural advantages and resources are such that we cannot long remain prostrate."[45]

As a result of the general downturn in the economy, Williams offered to sell his share of the partnership to Kilbourn. Like businessmen everywhere, he was desperately short of cash. Byron's response mirrored Milwaukee's depressed state of affairs. "Money with us is out of the question, and getting worse daily." Byron, and his fellow trustees on the west side, reduced taxes and issued their own bills of credit to pay manual laborers and provide a local medium of exchange. Specie in Milwaukee, as everywhere in the west, seemed to disappear overnight. As long as the prospect of making a quick profit on land sales in the city seemed likely, absentee speculators like Williams and Martin were interested. But once the economy declined, they wanted to bail out. Byron Kilbourn did not follow suit. Milwaukee had become his home, and he intended to remain there.

Like his father before him, Byron understood the importance of advertising. If newcomers were to be attracted to his settle-ment, they must first become aware of its advantages. In 1811, James Kilbourne had founded the *Western Intelligencer* to advertise the attractions of Worthington, Ohio. Twenty-five

62

years later, his son founded the *Milwaukee Advertiser* to do the same thing for his new town.

A.C. Wheeler tells us how a newspaper got started in that day: "the truth is, the first newspaper in a settlement is not demanded by the people. The intelligence is as yet centered in a few land holders, whose profits are prospective, and who hang all their dependence on immigration. The starting of a newspaper is speculation. The real estate needs an organ, and the heaviest man invests liberally in the nearest 'second hand' press, agrees to take a thousand copies of the sheet, and a journeyman printer is induced to try his fortune at the thing."

During a visit to Chicago late in 1835, Kilbourn made the acquaintance of D.H. Richards, a newcomer to that city who planned to buy the *Chicago Democrat*. Kilbourn persuaded Richards to visit Milwaukee first before making up his mind. The printer did so, and decided to move north and edit Milwaukee's first newspaper. Specifically designed to promote Kilbourntown, the *Milwaukee Advertiser* was six columns wide and four pages long. The initial print run was 1,200 copies. The paper was issued weekly, and later daily, for four and a half years. Dr. Lucius Barber, who didn't much care for Byron Kilbourn, liked his newspaper. Kilbourn he described as "a man of iron will, and strong prejudices, but never popular." The news weekly, he thought "really readable and well conducted."[46] Not to be out-done, Solomon Juneau established an east side rival in June 1837, the *Milwaukee Sentinel,* a form of which is still in print.

A different strategy that Byron used to advertise Kilbourn-town involved creating a copper plate map. Ostensibly, the map represented the entire Milwaukee area, but in actuality it "showed the platted portion all on the west side of the river ... with nothing on the east side but a marshy wilderness." Strangers were led to believe that the land east of the river was unfit for human habitation, and that if they chose to settle in Milwaukee, their future lay in Kilbourntown on the west side. In reality, at the time the map was issued, Juneautown had a larger population and a more prosperous business section than Kilbourntown. But first impressions are often hard to overcome, as Byron knew.[47]

Although Byron Kilbourn had arrived in Milwaukee in debt, he was full of hope. Within a year, he became solvent, and well on his way to wealth. He accomplished this by sacrificing his family, friends, and – some might say – values to the one goal of getting rich. He gambled that Milwaukee real estate would escalate in value, and he proved to be right. A witness to his father's development of Worthington a generation earlier, he knew how to proceed in developing a new community. He would surpass his rivals by outsmarting and outworking them, by seizing every opportunity that came his way, by the sheer force of his driving personality. While other speculators hoped to strike it rich and move on, Byron chose the path of hard work. At thirty-three, he recognized Milwaukee was his last opportunity to really make something of his life. He did not intend to fail. His apprenticeship in Ohio as a canal engineer equipped him to face the physical challenges the Milwaukee terrain had to offer. The presence of rival developers on the east side kept him eternally alert and active. In the crucial year of 1836, he must have struck his peers as a man possessed.

As Micajah Williams saw all too clearly, Kilbourn did not really understand the critical role politics could play in helping him achieve his goals. He thought it enough that his end was desirable; others should grasp that truth and simply follow his lead. Kilbourn was a man who had no time for small talk. He had no patience with opposition and delay. He was a man in a hurry to build a city. Once his mind was made up he seldom altered his course. More than either Solomon Juneau or George Walker, he compelled others to help him fulfill his dreams by sheer determination. Work took the place of everything else; he would leave no option untried that gave promise of his community's betterment. He seemed indifferent to whether he was well-liked. He had a mission to accomplish and he placed this above all else.

Byron's zeal to control others blinded him to the idea that he might achieve more in the end through persuasion. Increase Lapham said no town or city in the United States grew up with anything like the rapidity of Milwaukee. Byron Kilbourn played a major role in making this so. If you had a challenging task to accomplish, Kilbourn was your man. He got results quickly.

There were other sides to this driven man of business. For ten years he had been a husband, and he was a father as well as a businessman and community leader. Let us next turn to these facets of his personality.

Endnotes

[1] Cited in Bayrd Still*, Milwaukee: The History of a City* (Madison: State Historical Society of Wisconsin, 1948), p. 8.

[2] The following sources document the Juneau-Williams partnership: memo in the Martin Papers, Neville Public Museum, Green Bay, Wis.; "Narrative of Morgan L. Martin," *Collections*, SHSW, II (1888); Barbara Whalen, "The Lawyer and the Fur Trader: Morgan Martin and Solomon Juneau," *Milwaukee History* (Spring-Summer 1988), pp. 17-32; William J. Ewig, "The Business Career of Morgan L. Martin in Wisconsin, 1827-1850," unpublished master's thesis, University of Wisconsin-Milwaukee, Department of History, 1973.

[3] The authors are indebted to Harry Anderson, former executive director of MCHS, for allowing us to examine his notes on George Walker.

[4] Contemporary accounts of early Milwaukee include James S. Buck, *Pioneer History of Milwaukee, From the First American Settlement in 1833 to 1841, With a Topographical Description as it Appeared in a State of Nature* (4 vols., Milwaukee, Wis.: Swain and Tate, 1890), revised edition; "Story of Capt. William J. Donahoe, 1845-46," unpublished manuscript, Milwaukee Public Library, Milwaukee, Wisconsin (hereafter referred to as MPL); Edward D. Holton, "Commercial History of Milwaukee," *Collections*, SHSW (1904), 4, 274-279; Rudolph Koss, *Milwaukee*, Hans Ibsen trans., taken from the pages of the *Milwaukee Herold* in 1871. Of particular value are the insightful observations of Increase Lapham, Byron Kilbourn's knowledgeable business agent. Lapham published the first major book in the Wisconsin Territory, a data-filled geography. His letters to family members in Ohio are full of information for the period 1836-1840. See Lapham Papers, MCHS, SHSW, and OHC. In 1861, A. C. Wheeler interviewed Byron Kilbourn at length about the role he played in the founding of Milwaukee. *The Chronicles of Milwaukee: Being a Narrative History of the Town from its Earliest Period to the Present* (Milwaukee: Jermaine and Brightman, 1861). See especially pp. 74-75.

[5] Address to the Kilbourn Historical and Genealogical Society, SHSW, microfiche, August 20, 1854.

[6] For a life of Doty see Alice E. Smith, *James Duane Doty: Frontier Promoter* (Madison: State Historical Society of Wisconsin, 1954). Doty's offer to buy out the Juneau-Martin partnership is cited in Still, *Milwaukee*, p. 15.

[7] *Ibid*., p. 14, n. 36.

[8] "Narrative," pp. 405-406.

[9] Work began on a feeder canal between Lockbourne and Columbus in 1827. When the job was done four years later, the Kilbourns had laid out the town. Even though he failed in his attempt to locate the northern terminus of the Ohio Canal at Sandusky, James Kilbourne still hoped to profit from that

improvement. Berquist and Bowers, *The New Eden*, p. 200. Byron Kilbourn to Micajah Williams, May 19, 1835, OHC, Williams Papers, Box 3, Reel 3, Folder 1, Frames 095-096.

[10] *Ibid.*, pp. 17-19.

[11] Byron Kilbourn to James Kilbourn, January 23, 1836, OHC, Kilbourn Papers.

[12] Increase Lapham to Seneca Lapham, October 1, 1836, MCHS, Lapham Papers, Box 4, Folder 5.

[13] The figures cited here come from three sources: Louis B. Frank, *German-American Pioneers in Wisconsin and Michigan: The Frank-Kerler Letters, 1849-1864* (Milwaukee: Milwaukee County Historical Society, 1979), pp. 72-73; M. J. Springman and B. F. Guinan*, East Granby: The Evolution of a Connecticut Town* (Canaan, N.H.: Phoenix Publishing, 1983), p. 164; Mary Cowles Kilbourn to Glorianna Cowles, September 6, 1835, Cowles Family Papers.

[14] Mary Cowles Kilbourn to Glorianna Cowles, Cowles Family Papers. Note that both Byron and Mary named their daughters after their own biological mothers. They later named their sons after Byron and his maternal grandfather, John Fitch, rather than after Byron's father, James.

[15] B. H. Egerton to the editor of the *Milwaukee Sentinel*, September 25, 1877, ARC, UW-M, Bleyer Papers, Box 1. James Kilbourn to Whitfield Cowles, June 30, 1837, Cowles Family Papers.

[16] Mary Cowles Kilbourn to Whitfield Cowles, April 10, 1837; James Kilbourn to Whitfield Cowles, June 30, 1837, Cowles Family Papers. James's detailed letter regarding Mary's health in the last two years of her life and the events surrounding her death is especially informative. A clergyman writing to a fellow clergyman, James's words are graphic and solicitous. Byron was never close to his father-in-law and seldom wrote to him. His version of Mary's death appears in a letter he wrote to her brother, Rensselaer, June 24, 1837, Cowles Family Papers.

[17] The 9th was of course Kilbourntown. Increase Lapham to Darius Lapham, June 21, 1836, MCHS, Lapham Papers.

[18] *Milwaukee Sentinel,* July 16, 1839; A. W. Kellogg, "Life in Early Wisconsin," *Wisconsin Magazine of History*, 7:4 (June 1924), 484.

[19] Harry H. Anderson and Frederick I. Olson, *Milwaukee: At the Gathering of the Waters.* (Milwaukee: Milwaukee County Historical Society, 1981), p. 17.

[20] Letter printed in *Milwaukee Advertiser*, July 14, 1836.

[21] Kilbourn's "General Land Agency" is described in the first issue of the *Advertiser*, July 14, 1836.

[22] Autobiographical letter, I. Lapham to L. Draper, May 16, 1859, SHSW,

Lapham Papers; Graham Hawks, *Increase A. Lapham, Wisconsin's First Scientist*, published Ph.D. dissertation, University of Wisconsin Madison, Department of History, 1960. Lapham was a pioneer in half a dozen scientific fields and is often credited with being the "father" of the United States Weather Bureau.

[23] Will of Byron Kilbourn, July 17, 1868, MCHS.

[24] Byron Kilbourn to Micajah Williams, April 16, 1835, SHSW, Williams Papers; February 24, 1839, OHC, Williams Papers, Reel 3, Box 3, Folder 8.

[25] Increase Lapham to Micajah Williams, June 17, 1837, *ibid.*

[26] Increase Lapham to Darius Lapham, June 21, 1840, SHSW, Lapham Papers.

[27] Byron Kilbourn to Micajah Williams, December 5, 1836, SHSW, Williams Papers.

[28] Koss, *Milwaukee*, pp. 34-35.

[29] Roger D. Simon, "Foundations for Industrialization, 1835-1880," *Milwaukee History*, 12 (Spring-Summer 1978), 38-39.

[30] Koss, *Milwaukee,* pp. 41-42; E.H. Cleveland to D. W. Fowler, July 6, 1900, ARC, UW-M, Mss AO, Bleyer Papers, pp. 8-9.

[31] Buck, *Pioneer History*, 119; "Story," p. 8.

[32] Increase Lapham was still spending much of his time laying out streets and sidewalks nine years after Kilbourntown was founded. Increase Lapham to Darius Lapham, September 15, 1845, SHSW, typed letters, p. 16, MCHS, Box 4, Folder 6.

[33] Buck, *Pioneer History,* I, 86; Byron Kilbourn to Micajah Williams, February 27, 1837, SHSW, Williams Papers.

[34] Ray A. Sueflow, *A Plan for Survival* (New York, 1965).

[35] Herbert W. Kuhn, "Then Milwaukee Began to Build Its Own Ships," *Milwaukee History* I:1 (Autumn-Winter 1978), 61; *Milwaukee Advertiser*, July 8, September 16, 1837; H. Russell Austin, *The Milwaukee Story: The Making of an American City* (Milwaukee: The Journal Company, 1946), p. 53. Capt. Donahoe maintained that the Wisconsin Territory produced "the best ship building timber" in the country. "Story," p. 27. Koss, *Milwaukee*, p. 77. See also Wheeler, *Chronicles*, p. 231; Increase Lapham to Darius Lapham, July 30, 1840, MCHS, Lapham Papers, Box 4, Folder 6.

[36] MPL folder on steamship *Detroit; Milwaukee Advertiser*, June 24, July 1, 1837.

[37] I. Lapham, *A Geological and Topographical Description of Wisconsin: with Brief Sketches of its History, Geology, Mineralogy, Natural History, Population, Soil, Productions, Government Antiquities, etc,* (1844), p.140.

[38] *Milwaukee Advertiser*, July 14, 1836; August 31, 1839.

[39] Cowles Family Papers; *Milwaukee Advertiser*, July 14, 1836; July 1, 8, November 18, December 30, 1837; April 21, May 5, 1838; January 26, 1839.

[40] Joseph Schafer, "Origin of Wisconsin's Free School System," *Wisconsin Magazine of History* (1925-26), 32; Harry H. Anderson, "The First County Courthouse," *Historical Messenger*, December 1963, p. 101.

[41] Bray Hammond, *Banks and Politics in America -- From the Revolution to the Civil War* (Princeton: Princeton University Press, 1957), p. 455.

[42] Dr. Lucius J. Barber, "Recollections of Wisconsin, 1835-1839," OHC, Simsbury, Conn., Barber Papers, pp. 15-16.

[43] B. Kilbourn to M. Williams, May 7, 27, 1837, OHC, Williams Papers.

[44] Lapham to D. Lapham, September 27, 1837, MCHS, Lapham Papers.

[45] B. Kilbourn to I. H. Bronson, September 8, 1839, MCHS.

[46] Wheeler, *Chronicles*, pp. 58,60; John G. Gregory, *History of Milwaukee Wisconsin* (Chicago: S. J. Clarke, 1931), Vol. I, 110; "Recollections of Wisconsin, 1835-1839," Simsbury Historical Society (hereafter referred to as SHS), Barber Papers, pp. 16, 14.

[47] Edwin S. Mack, "The Founding of Milwaukee," *Proceedings*, SHSW (1906), p. 204; Still, *Milwaukee*, p. 23.

Kilbourn and Milwaukee

Mary's death forced Byron to take stock of himself. He had lost his beloved wife, and had two young daughters to raise. He needed a woman to be a mother for them and a wife for himself. A year after Mary died, he married Henrietta Kerrick of Baltimore, Maryland, an eastern beauty nine years his junior. Byron's new wealth guaranteed his new wife's having a houseful of servants. A succession of nannies came to care for Glorianna and Lucy.

Henrietta Kerrick, twenty-eight years old at the time she married Byron, was the youngest of five children of Joseph and

Early likeness of Henrietta Kerrick Kilbourn.

Rebecca Ord Kerrick of Baltimore. Byron and Henrietta met when Byron went to Washington to lobby for a land grant to help finance the building of the Milwaukee and Rock River Canal.

Described as "one of the men who helped build Baltimore," Joseph Kerrick had been a wealthy merchant. During the War of 1812, he helped underwrite the schooner *Baltimore*, and lost heavily when the British captured the vessel and confiscated its cargo. Kerrick's forwarding business failed in 1819; he left the city shortly thereafter, relocating in Philadelphia, where he died in 1829. Henrietta married Byron after a whirlwind courtship. Her personality was very different from that of Mary Cowles.

Contemporaries described the new Mrs. Kilbourn as pretty, aristocratic, and an "eastern belle" accustomed to money and servants.

Portrait of Henrietta Kerrick Kilbourn.

The three-story brick house at Chestnut and Third, originally intended for Mary, was already completed. With dimensions of 45 x 50 feet, the new house stood out among the smaller residential structures built west of the river. Byron and Henrietta were driven about the city in what the *Milwaukee Sentinel* called "a splendid barouche," a four-wheeled carriage with collapsible top, drawn by a pair of matched horses. Henrietta oversaw the rearing of Byron's two daughters. She also served as his hostess for social gatherings. And thirty-one months after their marriage, she presented him with a son and heir, Byron Hector. Five years later John Fitch, a second son, was added to the family.

While neighbors thought Henrietta conducted household affairs with propriety, she clearly enjoyed a good party, and late nights at the Kilbourns were often devoted to dancing, card playing, and music – leading to the rumor that the lady of the house was "somewhat dissipated in her habits."[1] A poor relative of Joel Buttles of Columbus who rented the Kilbourn house in 1845 spoke well of Byron, but had "many hard things" to say of Henrietta, whom he viewed as domineering and insensitive. A sister of Kilbourn's canal opponent, Harrison Reed of the *Sentinel*, described the second Mrs. Kilbourn as a person whose conduct was governed only by expediency – "principle she had none" – and reported that, after her marriage, she spent much of her time "in the nine pin alley." This same source told Mrs. Morgan Martin of Green Bay that the Kilbourns broke precedent, attending church together a half day before a county election in which Byron was a candidate.

That Henrietta's conduct as a bride did not win universal approval seems clear, but that she retained the affections of her husband is equally clear. Occasionally, she would accompany him on surveying trips to the interior, riding postillion at his side and, as she later recalled, in constant fear of Indian attack. As time went on, Henrietta engaged in those pursuits deemed more fitting the wife of one of Milwaukee's leading citizens. She provided aid to orphan children and collected funds to help the Mount Vernon Ladies Association purchase and restore the home of George

Washington. In 1845 she won a garden prize for her "pinks." But it was during the Civil War that she really came into her own. She collected funds to provide cheer for Union troops in training at Milwaukee's Camp Washburn, was a co-sponsor of the great soldiers fair of 1864, and assumed leadership of the newly-created Milwaukee Ladies Aid Society. In this latter role, Henrietta suggested the establishment of a federal soldiers' home at Milwaukee for troops who were sick, wounded, or destitute. This institution became the future Wood Veterans Hospital. With her son, Byron Hector, an infantry lieutenant at the front, she knew first hand the anxieties experienced by mothers back home, so she took the lead in ministering to the needs of those who served.

Perhaps it is only fitting that our final estimate of Henrietta should be that of her husband. Addressing Whitfield Cowles a year after the death of Mary, Byron wrote as follows: "I was married in Washington last Saturday a week ago, and have my

Byron Hector Kilbourn as a boy.

wife here. She is a young lady of good family, a good mind and well cultivated, and doubt not will make a good mother to the children of our dear departed Mary. My acquaintance with her was but short, having commenced since I came to Washington this spring but I was well satisfied with her disposition as a wife and mother, and took her by the hand for better or for worse."[2]

Byron Hector Kilbourn as a Lieutenant in the Union Army.

Unfortunately, we know comparatively little about Byron's children. Glorianna died at age fifteen, and Lucy Fitch followed the same year. Both died of tuberculosis, which was known as consumption. John Fitch died in 1850, at age five, leaving only Byron Hector to carry on the family name. Heir to a sizable fortune, Byron Hector received a first-class education. He began his schooling in Milwaukee, then transferred to the Cheshire Academy, an Episcopal preparatory school in Connecticut. He went on to Yale as an undergraduate, and later studied medicine in Chicago and Louisville. During the Civil War, his regiment, the Third Wisconsin, saw action in Virginia, Pennsylvania, Tennessee, and Georgia.

When the war ended, Byron Hector spent several years managing a coffee plantation in Guatemala until "one of the innumerable political revolutions made it expedient for citizens of the United States to leave that country." Upon completion of his medical degree, he spent several years in practice in Milwaukee.

He then retired to a fine home he had built at North Lake, west of the city. He named his estate "Hawkhurst," after the Kilbourn's ancestral homestead in Kent, England. Byron Hector became a country gentleman and a pillar of the local Episcopal Church, providing much-needed financial support and serving as a lay reader.[3]

Byron Kilbourn's attention was not, however, upon his son but upon his business affairs; it was Henrietta's job to oversee the activities of the children. In Ohio, Lucy Fitch, Byron's stepmother Cynthia Barnes, and three older sisters ran the household. In Wisconsin, Mary Cowles, Henrietta Kerrick, and a series of servants served in this role, ministering to the needs of both husband and children.

Nineteenth-century business leaders were expected, as they are today, to devote a portion of their time and resources to civic affairs. Byron Kilbourn was a case in point. We know, of course, that he served on a variety of boards and committees. He also donated land to the city for a west side market, an elementary school, and a park. One of these plots later became the site for Milwaukee's 1400-seat Academy, "the most complete public hall for dramatic purposes west of Philadelphia."[4]

Byron's role in the local chapter of the Free Masons was particularly noteworthy. Like James before him, he helped establish a Masonic lodge, the third to be chartered in the Wisconsin Territory. Gordon Wood reminds us, the Masons were "probably the single most important fraternal and benevolent society of the early republic.... Freemasonry was, in fact, something of a surrogate religion for many Americans." Byron, who never became a member of an established church, became a faithful member of the local chapter. In the fall of 1843, he assisted thirty-eight others in establishing Milwaukee's first Masonic lodge. In the years that followed, he was repeatedly elected Worthy Master (lodge leader) and in 1859, he generously provided the chapter with a permanent home. The second and third floors of a building he owned on North Third Street were deeded over to the lodge for this purpose, and the resulting facility was "said to be a fairer hall than any of the kind in the West." In recognition of Byron's gift, the chapter was renamed "Kilbourn Lodge No. 3," a name it bears to this day.

When Byron died in 1870, his lodge brothers were quick to recognize his many contributions. They noted that he "assisted in the organization of this lodge in the year 1843, and has ever since been an earnest, unselfish worker for its prosperity." Nearing death, Byron funded "a general library of science, literature and the arts," to be housed at the lodge hall. His tribute concludes with the observation that "in his relation to the lodge and its members, Brother Kilbourn was just and resolute and none of us could ever doubt the correctness of his judgment. In his intercourse with its members, and particularly, with the younger brethren, his conversation was entertaining and peculiarly instructive, and we

Masonic portrait of Byron Kilbourn.

rarely left him without having learned some lessons of wisdom."[5] Kilbourn outlived both Solomon Juneau and George Walker. Partly in consequence, he became a kind of elder statesman in Milwaukee, readily recalling the epic events that shaped the community's early development.

Kilbourn's involvement with civic affairs had two other dimensions: fire prevention and higher education. As noted earlier, Milwaukee grew up almost overnight. In its haste to be first, most of its buildings, residential and business, were made of wood, locally available in plentiful supply. The danger of fire, especially in the drier seasons, was everpresent. In April of 1845, a major fire destroyed $90,000 worth of property on East Water Street between Michigan and Huron. Only a third of the loss was covered by insurance, and investigators concluded the tragedy was due primarily to inadequate firefighting equipment. In the early years citizens depended upon volunteer fire companies to protect them. Each resident was required to have two buckets of water handy at all times. But there was no central department, and equipment was primitive at best. Consequently,

Byron Kilbourn's residence at Fourth and Wisconsin.

fire prevention was a frequent agenda topic for the Milwaukee Common Council.

In the summer of 1846, two costly fires took place within a mile of Kilbourn's house. The first involved the Perkins Machine Shop, and the second, the Chase/Comstock Mill, located alongside the Rock River Canal. Arson was suspected. As a conscientious alderman for the second ward, Byron took a personal interest in these developments. He moved that the Common Council offer a $500 reward for information leading to the capture of the arsonist. His second motion mandated the return of property taxes to the victims of the fire, and proposed the appointment of additional night watchmen for the second ward. The gutted mill was owned by Cicero Comstock, an old friend from Worthington days. On his own, Byron donated $100 for the use of local volunteer firemen.

In 1854, during his second term as mayor, Byron discussed the problem of recent fires and expense of reconstruction. Declaring that "fire fighting was the entire community's responsibility," he criticized "pedestrian idleness" during a recent conflagration. He also noted with disdain "the practice of serving liquor to working firemen and offering money for the rescue of particular property.... Stringent measures should be taken against offenders," he declared. Kilbourn personally offered $500 for the arrest of those arsonists responsible for the destruction. Two years later, fire struck Kilbourn's own elegant townhouse on Spring Street, now Wisconsin Avenue. Under the heading "Narrow Escape," the *Sentinel* printed the following notice: "The large and handsome residence of Byron Kilbourn, Esq., on Spring Street in the 4th ward, narrowly escaped destruction by fire yesterday afternoon. Thro' some defect in the flues of the Hot Air Furnace, the joists and flooring of a room on the lower floor took fire, and but for the timely assistance of some passers by, the whole building would probably have been burnt. As it was, vigorous efforts, and a copious supply of water, extinguished the fast rising flames." On June 26, 1861, the same residence was hit by lightning, but again a quick response limited the damage.

View of Kilbourn Park Reservoir

Adequate water supply was a key problem in fighting fires. Although house fires might be contained if discovered early, such was seldom the case with larger buildings. Given Byron's personal experience with fires, we should not be surprised to learn that he devised an appropriate solution. Having first donated the site of his proposed university to the city as a park, he then recommended that a reservoir be established to provide the city with a guaranteed water supply sufficient for any emergency. His proposal, made in August of 1867, was favorably received. A central water system was established in 1873, and five years later the Milwaukee Reservoir, which exists to this day, was given the official name of "Kilbourn Park."[6]

A lesser-known but revealing chapter in Byron's Milwaukee career involved the establishment of a university. In January 1858, Kilbourn requested a charter from the state legislature to establish a new institution of higher learning in Milwaukee. The site was to be a fifteen-acre plot of land located on the north side, in Milwaukee's sixth ward. The land abutted North Avenue and was so elevated as to afford a fine view of the river, the city, and the Lake Michigan shoreline. Byron said he intended to donate the site and to will the bulk of his considerable real estate in Milwaukee County to the support of the new institution. At the time, his holdings were estimated to be worth $500,000 (or about $7 million in current currency). "Kilbourn University" was designed to provide tuition-free instruction to the sons of poor parents, regardless of religion. Preference was to be given to orphans, and enrollees were eligible from anywhere in the state. Four trustees, including Increase Lapham, were to run the institution, and it was the donor's expectation that the institution would be self-supporting. Kilbourn made his proposal to the legislature, as it was the one body within the state empowered to grant a charter. The Kilbourn home at Fourth and Wisconsin was to be excluded from this proposal. This residential property was to be turned over to the City of Milwaukee, rented, and the proceeds used to support the city's poor. Lapham sent a copy of Kilbourn's plan to his friend in Boston, Charles Sergeant, for reaction. Sergeant thought the idea "noble," and likened it to Stephen Girard's generous endowment of a similar institution in Philadelphia. He also applauded the timeliness of Kilbourn's action: "every generous spirit will sympathize with his desire of 'doing something' for the furtherance of the work while life with its energies still remains."

The Kilbourn University bill was opposed in the legislature on three counts: first, the dominant role Byron reserved for himself in the establishment of the new institution; second, the proposal of tax exemption for an institution of higher learning; and third, the fact that the author of the proposal was Byron Kilbourn. At the time Kilbourn was unpopular in much of the state because of the efforts he used to win legislative approval for a railroad land grant. Byron argued that his university should be tax free due to its benevolent statewide mission. Some lawmakers favored a much more limited one-time exemption of $50,000. For five months the bill ran its course. In the state Senate, the committee of the whole endorsed the proposal by a vote of 17 to 9 on February 24, 1858. But the Assembly refused to budge from the amendments it wanted. So on May 6 the proposal was "indefinitely postponed"; opponents viewed Kilbourn University as a "vast monied corporation without suitable restrictions." Had the proposer been anyone other than Byron Kilbourn, the bill might have passed. Undoubtedly, the members of the legislature were influenced by a concurrent land grant investigation. At one point in the negotiations, the Senate instructed the joint investigating committee to determine whether deeds to "corner lots" at Kilbourn City – the present Wisconsin Dells where Byron had a large amount of property – had been offered to any members of the legislature to influence their vote.

Typical of the opposition at the time was an editorial printed in Madison's *Daily State Journal*: Byron Kilbourn needed no monument to himself, as "the name of the man who 'propitiated' the Executive and Legislative departments of Government is not likely to be forgotten." Resorting to bitter satire, the *Journal* predicted Kilbourn himself would become "Chancellor" of the new university "and lecture on the morality of bribery when necessary." In a succeeding issue, the Journal went so far as to propose that the new state penitentiary at Waupun be renamed in Kilbourn's honor.

A quite different view of the proposed institution was provided by the *Milwaukee Sentinel*:

> In the Senate yesterday, Mr. Greulich of this city, introduced a memorial from Byron Kilbourn, Esq., asking a charter for "Kilbourn University." This is the incipient step of a great Educational Enterprise. Mr. Kilbourn, we learn, has set apart some 15 acres in the Sixth Ward, on the high ground over-looking the river, near the Round House of the La Crosse R. R. for the uses and purposes of the University. He designs, besides endowing it to the amount of several hundred thousand dollars, intending the endowment to be sufficient to admit of Board, as well as Tuition, being furnished, free of cost, to all scholars attending the University. Suitable buildings will be erected on the chosen

site, which is a commanding and eligible one, and the management of the University will be confided to a Board of Trustees. – Connected to the University will be an Astronomical Observatory of the first class, to be provided with all the necessary apparatus. In short, it is the intention of Mr. Kilbourn to make this a University in fact as well as in name. Such an institution will be a noble and enduring monument to the enlightened public spirit and munificent liberality of its founder.

The decision of the Assembly on May 6 to postpone the bill indefinitely did not terminate Kilbourn's interest in the project. On October 11 he asked formal permission of the Milwaukee Common Council to reserve the site for a university. Kilbourn indicated that adjacent land would be added to the fifteen-acre parcel once the institution received its charter. On January 11, 1859, he resubmitted his plan to the legislature.

It is not known precisely when Kilbourn gave up the idea, but on March 14, 1859, Increase Lapham wrote him about funding any one of three ambitious alternatives: a new institution modeled after the Smithsonian Institution in Washington, D.C., a large public library, or a museum of natural history.[7] Four days later Byron responded as follows: "I think very highly of the recommendations submitted by you, but cannot at present determine in relation to them. Being at Kilbourn City recently, I mentioned the idea of establishing a labour school there, which they highly approved, and though not committed fully to that project, the people there would feel disappointed if I should wholly abandon it. There is however time for reflection, and I will see you further on the subject."[8] Perhaps the war delayed further action on Kilbourn's part. Whatever the reason, none of these three proposals was ultimately funded. In the end, Kilbourn's efforts to establish a Milwaukee university proved unsuccessful.

Let us turn now to a different project, one Byron Kilbourn championed for the dozen years Wisconsin was a territory – the

Milwaukee and Rock River Canal. Would this man, whom Micajah Williams viewed as "an engineer of ability, courage and integrity," achieve his objective in this venture?[9] Or would his failure to grasp the importance of practical politics negate his best efforts to create in Wisconsin what he helped achieve in Ohio?

Endnotes

[1] The Wisconsin territorial census of 1836 lists ten members of the Kilbourn household, only four of whom were family members. Probably Increase Lapham was among this number as he stayed with the Kilbourns when he first came to Milwaukee in July. R. G. Thwaites, "First Territorial Census," *Collections*, SHSW. 13:268 (1908). The federal census of 1850 lists the Kilbourns as having two maids and one man servant. *Milwaukee Sentinel*, July 10, 1838. Joel Buttles's diary, June 19, 1845, OHC; Gary L. Browne, *Baltimore in the Nation, 1789-1861* (Chapel Hill: University of North Carolina Press, 1980), p. 80.

[2] B. Kilbourn to W. Cowles, June 24, 1838, Cowles Family Letters.

[3] *Milwaukee Sentinel* May 9, September 10, 1850; Buttles's diary, November 8, 1845; Louis F. Frank, *The Medical History of Milwaukee, 1834-1914* (Milwaukee: Germania Publishing Company, 1915), p. 64; Frank L. Klement, *Wisconsin and the Civil War* (Stevens Point, Wis.: Worzalla Publishing Co., 1963), *passim*; Gregory, History of *Milwaukee Wisconsin,* II, 969; *History of Waukesha County* (Chicago: Western Historical Co., 1880), pp. 751-752; Harold E. Wagner, *The Episcopal Church in Wisconsin - 1847-1947* (Waterloo, Wis.: Courier Printing Co., 1947), p. 238.

[4] Wheeler, *Chronicles*, p. 285. This building was later replaced by a much larger structure known as the Milwaukee Auditorium.

[5] Gordon S. Wood, ed., *The Rising Glory of America, 1760-1820* (Boston: Northeastern University Press, rev. ed., 1990), p. 90; Wheeler, *Chronicles*, pp. 284-285; *Milwaukee Sentinel*, January 12, 1871.

[6] Lapham, *Wisconsin*, p.116; Louise P. Kellogg, "The Origin of Milwaukee College*,"* *Wisconsin Magazine of History*, 9:4 (1925-26), 389; *Milwaukee Sentinel*, February 15, 1854, March 13, 1855, January 16, 1857, June 26, 1861; M. E. Lightbourne, "E. B. Howland and Early Fire Fighting in Milwaukee," *Historical Messenger* (September 1965), p. 66; Kilbourn's council resolution on behalf of the Chase/Comstock Company, *Record, 1846-48*, vol. I, City of Milwaukee, 98-100. As mayor in 1854, Kilbourn made several recommendations for improving fire prevention; see *Milwaukee Sentinel*, August 28, September 11.

[7] Box 5 of the Lapham Papers at SHSW contains a number of items regarding Kilbourn University. See especially C. Sargent to Increase Lapham, February 2, 1858; Senator J. Sutherland to Increase Lapham, February 4, 1858; Increase Lapham to his ten-year-old son, March 15, 1858. For the bill's progress through the legislature see *Senate Journal*, vol. I, Wisconsin, Jan.-Mar. 1858 and *Journal of the Assembly*, Feb.-Mar. 1858. For the extremes of press

reaction, see *Milwaukee Sentinel*, January 15, 1858 and *Daily State Journal* (Madison), January 16 and March 5, 1858, January 18, 1859. Lapham's suggestions for educational alternatives are contained in a letter to Kilbourn dated March 14, 1859.

[8] SHSW, Lapham Papers, Box 5.

[9] Samuel M. Williams, "Micajah Terrell Williams – A Sketch." *Wisconsin Magazine of History*, VI (1922-23), 310.

The Milwaukee and Rock River Canal

Byron Kilbourn was first and foremost a man of business. While his grief for Mary in the summer of 1837 was genuine, it was short-lived. A hundred tasks demanded his attention in Milwaukee, and he returned to Wisconsin as soon as he could arrange for his daughters' care at Worthington.

On July 7, he wrote a revealing letter to his Worthington friend, Cicero Comstock.[1] The letter was sent from the S. S. *Michigan*, then departing Green Bay for Milwaukee. The largest vessel sailing on the Great Lakes, the *Michigan* was considered the height of luxury in its day, with a paneled and gilded dining room, staterooms, and an elegantly appointed ladies cabin. There were 118 passenger births aboard, plus additional room in steerage for the less affluent. Reveling in his "forced vacation" from the frenzy of Milwaukee, Byron described the fare as "sumptuous ... fresh fish every day in the greatest perfection I ever saw them," including "gigantic Mackinaw trout."

The Steamship Michigan, *the largest passenger vessel on the Great Lakes in its day.*

The remarkable thing about Kilbourn's letter is its tone. It is as if the carefree bachelor of an earlier era reappears, as if Byron had closed one chapter in his life and was ready to embark on another. There is a lightheartedness to his sentences, and no reference at all to Mary, or his grief, or the children, or James Kilbourn, Jr., Byron's stepbrother, who traveled with him.[2] Instead, the emphasis is upon describing his fellow passengers and thoughts about the Worthington friends he had just left. If the reader were unaware of Mary's tragic death three weeks earlier, Byron's letter would seem simply the account of an observant traveler.

The Milwaukee Kilbourn was returning to was in a rapid state of change. Earlier, in the space of two short years, the town had grown from three log cabins and a half dozen inhabitants to 200 buildings and 1,200 residents. "Our town is improving as rapidly as the supply of lumber will allow," Increase Lapham reported.[3] In the history of Milwaukee, 1836 was a banner year. James Buck explains why:

> The tide of immigration had now commenced to flow into the embryo city like a river; speculation was rife; every man's pocket was full of money; lots were selling with a rapidity and for prices that made those who bought or sold them feel like Vanderbilt. Buildings went up like magic, three days being all that was wanted, if the occupant was in a hurry, in which to erect one. Stocks of goods would be sold out in many instances before they were fairly opened, and at an enormous profit. Everyone was sure his fortune was made, and a stiffer-necked people, as far as prospective wealth was concerned, could not be found in America. Nothing like it was ever seen before; no western city had such a birth. People were dazed at the rapidity of its growth; all felt good. The wonderful, go-aheadativeness of the American people was in full blast; neither was it checked for the entire

season. Some sixty buildings were erected, many of them of goodly dimensions. Streets were graded, ferries established, officers of the law appointed, medical and agricultural societies formed, a court house and jail erected, and all in five short months.[4]

As the compiler of a city directory later observed, "Unlike Chicago, Detroit, and other now flourishing lake cities, Milwaukee had no prolonged childhood existence, but, as if impatient of an infantile state, struggled into manhood" with astonishing speed, "almost unparalleled in the world's history."[5]

Speculators flooded the community. State banks issued notes worth "many times their specie reserve" – a practice which resulted in even more loans for investors. "Sales of public lands leaped" from four million acres in 1834 to twelve million in 1835, and "an all time high" of twenty million in 1836, "with Michigan [including the lands west of the lake] leading all states and territories in sales this last year.... The increasing investment in land had a self-accelerating effect by attracting others who had observed profits being taken, and by banks, loaning monies deposited by government land offices to land speculators."[6]

Faced with these dynamic conditions, Byron Kilbourn made money in three ways. First, he would buy a section of land cheaply, subdivide it, and then sell it off in individual lots for a substantial profit. Second, he would lend money to a buyer to cover the down payment for a piece of property. The borrower was charged seven percent per annum for a short-term loan of three to five years. If the borrower later defaulted on his payments, as many did in the aftermath of the Panic of 1837, the property, along with whatever improvements had been made, reverted to Kilbourn, who was then free to resell it to someone else. In the 1840s and 1850s, Kilbourn's attorney often appeared in court to sue borrowers for non-payment of their loans.[7] Third, and certainly the easiest way to make money, he would hold property until demand increased prices. Increase Lapham noted that town lots could be purchased for a tenth down, "and the remainder in thirds over three years."[8] Thus, a lot for sale at $1,000, could be bought for $100, with three subsequent payments of $300 each. Everyone assumed rising prices would easily cover later payments. In 1835-36, quick profits appeared so much a certainty that an east side surveyor told his father, "I can say to you with utmost confidence that I have no doubt but what I can clear 100 per cent in four to six months...100 per cent every year at the least calculation.... I never have known of an instance when the purchaser lost money."[9] With odds like these, who could resist?

Migrants to the Wisconsin Territory in 1837 were a mixed lot; most had little money. Kilbourn described those he encountered on shipboard at Green Bay:

> You have of course some Experience in the motley character of the multitude constituting the passengers of a steamboat, but yet such a collection of Tom, Dick, Dutch and the devil I presume you never did see as we have had on board. The wilds of the northwest and the great tide of western emigration were required to unite in order to form it, and as found it is rare I tell you beyond description. We have first, Americans from every conceivable direction; second, several Indians, old and young, and of both sexes, third, 2 half breeds, ladies of high cultivation, and wives of genteel men in the region, 4th, some specimens of French, 5th, several niggers, 6th, several Irish, 7th, a large number of Norwegians of both sexes & all ages, and decidedly the most degraded set of beings whom I ever saw, 8thly, the devil knows what.[10]

What is missing from this account is any reference to newcomers from Germany. The first wave of these would arrive at Milwaukee two years later, in 1839.

Unlike the Norwegians Kilbourn observed at Green Bay, Milwaukee's Germans tended to be conservative people of modest means. Most of them were agricultural workers, crowded off farms by overpopulation. Faced with few prospects at home, they were anxious to better themselves abroad. Willing to work long and hard to get ahead, these sturdy Germans were unlike the Yankee speculators who preceded them: they had no illusions about instant wealth. Instead, they sought to achieve their goals through thrift and hard work. The following example taken from rural Illinois typifies Milwaukee's newcomers: "a German Immigrant...hired himself out to an American farmer...to chop wood. The German worked for $6 per month, helping the American clear his farmland. By the time the American farmer had depleted his financial resources, the German had saved $300 from his wages, which he then used to purchase the farm from his former employer." If a new arrival could save a little money, he "could look forward to profits even in the first year."[11]

The first German immigrants left their homeland for economic reasons, though later arrivals were motivated by the desire for religious or political freedom. The majority chose to live in Kilbourntown, settling along the river between Chestnut Street and North Avenue. They did so for practical reasons: First, Juneau's east side was already largely built up. Yankees and Yorkers occupied the heights, leaving only the less desirable lowlands for newcomers. Second, the populous east side had little room for expansion while Kilbourntown possessed limitless possibilities. Also, west side lots tended to be smaller and cheaper. Most important of all, the west side offered opportunities for immediate employment, first, in the construction of a dam and canal, and later, at sawmills, gristmills, and tanneries – industries which sprang up once a steady supply of water power was assured. Those who lived on the west side could easily walk to work. They filled the city's need for an increasing supply of reliable workers. The German settlement on the west side "became known as the 'Gartenstadt' (garden city), for its little houses with fenced-in gardens, displaying lovely flowers, and in the back of the house...little vegetable plots."[12] "Legend has it," a Milwaukee journalist noted, "that some stores had signs in their windows reading 'English Spoken Here', in the hope of attracting occasional patrons from other parts of town."[13]

German migration began as a trickle, became a stream, and then a flood. By the early 1840s, arrivals "averaged 1200 per week in ice-free months." By 1850, fully one-third of Milwaukee's 45,000 citizens were either born in Germany or of German extraction.[14] No one grasped the implications of this German "invasion" more quickly than Byron Kilbourn. His first move was especially shrewd. He gave a free building lot near his home to a well-to-do "Old Lutheran," who then proceeded to erect a handsome, half-timbered house on it...as an example of how a house should be built.[15] Almost immediately, a host of his countrymen followed suit, wishing to reside nearby. Of course, they purchased their land from Byron Kilbourn. Kilbourn arranged to have the governor's address to the legislature printed in German, a first in the history of the territory. He negotiated German political support for the measures of the Democratic Party, with the help of Dr. Franz Huebschmann. He was the principal speaker at a rally held at the "German" market to protest European repression of liberalism. And when a German count decided to found his own community in interior Wisconsin, the nobleman cleverly installed his land agent in an office across the street from Kilbourn's house.[16]

Incoming Germans preferred to settle among their own, and soon the second ward on Kilbourn's side of the river became known as "the German Ward." James Buck described the boost these new settlers gave to the city: "The...arrival of these hardy sons of toil, with their gold and silver wherewith to purchase homes for themselves and their children...was electric."[17] In the aftermath of the depression of 1837, settlers with money "to invest in land, equipment and supplies" were welcome, regardless of the place of their birth.

As noted earlier, Byron Kilbourn was convinced Milwaukee's economy would improve in time. But he was not the kind of person to stand idly by waiting for this to happen. What was needed was a stimulus, some fresh incentive to fuel the economy. Early Milwaukeeans dreamed of a railroad to link their city with the Mississippi, but railroads, even short ones, were costly to build, and money for internal improvements was virtually non-existent in the new Wisconsin Territory. Nationally, railroads were in their infancy, with only a handful of functioning lines in the whole country. What lines existed were short and concentrated on the east coast. The era of the steam locomotive would not come to Wisconsin for another fifteen years, when Byron Kilbourn built the state's first line. A transcontinental road would not be constructed until four years after the Civil War ended.

But a canal was quite a different proposition.

New York's Erie Canal opened for business in 1825, quickly demonstrating to all that water transportation could be both economical and profitable. Of course, no one needed to make this point to Byron Kilbourn, for he had played a key role in the construction of Ohio's flourishing canal system. The idea of a waterway to connect the Great Lakes with the Mississippi was hardly new. This, after all, was the aim of the two canals Kilbourn had worked on in Ohio, along with several projected in Indiana and Illinois. The territory's first newspaper, *The Green Bay Intelligencer*, noted that a Milwaukee Rock River Canal project was under discussion as early as the fall of 1835, and at Milwaukee's first public meeting, on December 17, Albert Fowler proposed that Wisconsin's new territorial council authorize its construction.[18] In the beginning, everyone in Milwaukee seemed to favor the idea.

The Wisconsin Territory was formally established July 3, 1836, and its first legislature convened the following fall. To prepare for this event, Byron Kilbourn assembled a surveying crew (including the newly arrived Increase Lapham), and spent the summer investigating possible routes. Experienced canal engineers, Kilbourn and Lapham, found no major barriers to

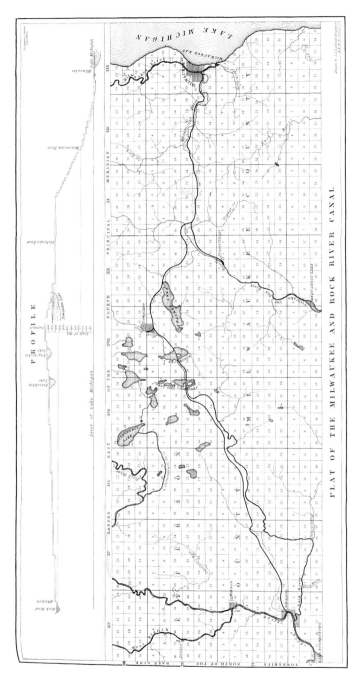

*Plat of the Milwaukee & Rock River Canal
drawn by Increase Lapham.*

construction. They thought the cost would be "moderate."[19] Keep in mind that the population of the entire Wisconsin Territory numbered fewer than 23,000 whites in September of 1836. Most of these lived in Green Bay, Milwaukee, Racine, and in the lead district at Mineral Point. There were only six organized counties in the territory, spread in a diagonal line from Washington Island in the northeast to Prairie du Chien in the southwest. About three-fourths of the future state of Wisconsin had no white residents at all.

Just as Buffalo and Cleveland had become important seaports because of canal construction, now it was Milwaukee's turn. Supporters argued that a canal would spur agricultural development because it would guarantee farmers access to markets for surplus crops. Miners were told they could cut their shipping costs in half if such a waterway were built. According to the *Milwaukee Sentinel*, the canal would facilitate "trade and business of a farming interior as fertile as the delta of the Nile, and a mineral region of more real value than the mines of Peru."[20] Eastern manufactured goods would become readily available with a canal, and at Milwaukee, Kilbourn and Williams envisioned a dam to supply water power for new industry.[21] Commerce and industry, together, would ensure Milwaukee's prosperity, a prosperity that would surely increase the value of their property. The dream of imminent greatness was contagious. Everyone – at least every Milwaukeean – applauded the canal idea at first, though no one was quite clear how the project was to be funded.

The first step in making the dream a reality involved legislative approval for the formation of a private canal company. Wisconsin's first territorial legislature met at Belmont in Lafayette County in November and December 1836. At this session, an incorporation bill, drafted by Byron Kilbourn, was introduced, but it seems the lawmakers had more pressing business to attend to as they struggled to establish a government for their newly created territory. Undeterred, Kilbourn pressed forward. Between May 20 and June 17 of 1837, he published a series of five lengthy essays in the *Milwaukee Advertiser*, designed to explain the importance and feasibility of the proposed waterway. He described the details of construction, and stressed the important benefits to come to the citizens of the territory: reduced transportation costs, and ready access to markets. "All these matters were considered," a territorial historian noted, "and placed in a favorable point of view."[22]

Increase Lapham was sent west to the Rock River, in Jefferson County, to make a precise estimate of building costs. He planned a waterway no less than four feet deep, approximately fifty-two miles in length, with a series of locks and dams for water power and changing elevations, the whole to be connected to an already existing chain of rivers and lakes. Once westward traffic reached the Rock River, it could either proceed south to the Mississippi by way of the Illinois River, or travel west through the Four Lakes at Madison, and on to the Wisconsin River. Lapham estimated the project would cost about $800,000.[23] Kilbourn told Micajah Williams in November of 1837 that "passage of a canal bill ... will give us a lift," for such a law would surely increase the value of land in Milwaukee and along the canal route.[24]

When the territorial legislature met again in 1837, Kilbourn's bill was reintroduced. This time it passed, and Kilbourn's new friend from the lead country, Governor Henry Dodge, signed it into law on January 5, 1838. "Our next great object," Byron reported to Williams, "is to secure the means to carry it into operation. There is, in our legislature, a great fear of incorporations in general, and it had required a great deal of care and attention, as well as time, to obtain the passage of this act, although so obviously beneficial to the whole eastern territory if carried into effect. I have, in addition, to this general indisposition to grant charters, to contend with Racine jealousy, and still worse, the underhand opposition of our own representative in the Council [Alanson Sweet]. Putting these obstacles all together, it has required five weeks to accomplish what I thought could be done in two...."[25] This last statement must have brought a smile to Williams' face, for he was the one who earlier had tried to alert Byron to his ignorance of politics.

Alanson Sweet opposed Kilbourn's canal because he suspected Byron was trying to enrich himself at the expense of canal settlers. At issue was the cost of land along the canal route. Usually the government sold its land for $1.25 per acre, but in the bill authorizing the canal land grant, Congress stipulated that this figure be doubled to $2.50 an acre. Irate settlers claimed their "right" to the lower price had been violated. They held Kilbourn and his company responsible. At Belmont, and later at Washington, D.C., Sweet tried unsuccessfully to block the canal project.

A second issue divided the two Milwaukeeans. A "Bank of Milwaukee" was created by the legislature November 30, 1836. Sweet was a key player, naming four of the bank's directors, as well as its cashier. On February 2, 1839, the Secretary of the Treasury appointed Byron Kilbourn one of two examiners to look into the affairs of the new institution. Sweet at once viewed Kilbourn as his enemy, and even though his bank never actually opened its doors, he remained a loud opponent of the canal.

A crowd burned Sweet in effigy in 1837, and Kilbourn vented his anger against his opponent in vitriolic speeches, and newspaper editorials. Although unable to stop the canal, Sweet's opposition divided the Democratic Party in Wisconsin, with Harrison Reed of the *Sentinel*, and Judge Doty of Green Bay, heading a new anti-canal, anti-Kilbourn faction. This anti-canal group became strong enough to elect Doty over Kilbourn in the race for delegate to Congress in 1839.[26]

On February 2, 1837, canal stock was put on sale at Kilbourn's business office in Milwaukee; $100,000 was quickly subscribed. On the seventh, the first meeting of the newly formed company was held. The board of directors promptly named Kilbourn, president, and Lapham, engineer. A set of Kilbourn-drafted bylaws was approved, and the directors passed a Kilbourn-drafted resolution to Congress, proposing a land grant with which to fund canal construction. Money represented Kilbourn's greatest problem. He could count on the good wishes of most of the people of Milwaukee and the support of the

Democratic-controlled legislature, plus a friendly governor. But no one within the territory was in a position to fund so sizable an undertaking. If the canal were to be built, the money must be secured elsewhere, either from the federal government or from eastern capitalists. Or a combination of both. The federal treasury in Washington was empty, but the government had millions of acres of land at its disposal. If Byron Kilbourn could secure a grant of land along the route of the canal, as others had been able to do in other western states, the cost of construction might be defrayed through the sale of property.

"It is a subject of the very first importance to our interests to secure an appropriation of land at this session," Kilbourn wrote Williams, as it will lend "character" to our "enterprise, which will be lost by delay" beyond the time of the upcoming land sales which had been scheduled for 1839.[27] If Congress should agree to the grant, "all secondary questions will be definitely settled; all diversity of opinion (as *the great point*) on the west shore of Lake Michigan will evaporate, and those little questions of great importance at home, will be disposed of without any further struggle."

On February 24, Kilbourn notified Williams that $100,000 of canal company stock had been spoken for, and that the company was now formally organized, with "a good and efficient board of directors, myself, as president." Earlier Byron suggested the appropriate appointees to the governor. The land grant, Byron wrote, is "a question of more importance to our interest than has been or probably ever will be presented to us.... By united and aggressive effort we can succeed in getting an appropriation. This done its completion will be rendered certain and can be done in a very short time." In many ways the canal project was a monument to the efforts of one man, Byron Kilbourn.

Kilbourn claimed that opinion within the territory "is all in its favor, & it only wants the means, wch I think are within our reach, to give our place in the recent instance that importance wch it is entitled to ultimately, but wch in the ordinary course of things it may take a long time to attain." Acquiring the canal grant will settle "definitely and forever all questions of local doubt and difficulty among the points of business there."[28]

In order to secure congressional support, the board of directors authorized Kilbourn to go to Washington to act as lobbyist. In early March of 1838, after an eight-day trip by sleigh from Milwaukee, Byron arrived in Worthington.[29] He was met there by his partner, Williams, and the two left together by stage for the east. At Washington, the Milwaukee and Rock River Canal bill was introduced by Senator Clement Comer Clay of Alabama on behalf of the Senate Committee on Public Lands. At Byron's request, Wisconsin's territorial delegate, George W. Jones, presented the company resolution to the members of Congress. Kilbourn's mission involved persuasion, both in public and behind the scenes. On May 31, he distributed a circular to congressmen designed to explain the attitude of squatters on canal lands. "I know the anxiety of the people for the accomplishment of this object to be very great, in that section of the country that would be affected most; and I do not hesitate to say, if left to a vote of themselves, whether to increase the price of the alternate sections, or fail in the appropriation for the canal, their voice would be unanimous for the increase. Many of them, within my own knowledge, would prefer to pay five dollars an acre, rather than forego [sic] the advantages which the canal would be to them, and to the country at large."

Byron's rhetoric exceeded the bounds of prudence. Fortunately, Congress did not follow his thinking or raise the price to $5 an acre (more than three times the normal cost of government land). But they did settle for $2.50, thereby ensuring that the return on the sale of canal land would equal that of both odd and even sections, had they been sold at $1.25 per acre. Senator James Buchanan of Pennsylvania fathered an amendment that excluded the right of preemption for the first settlers on canal land. Between late March and early June, Kilbourn spent much of his time meeting with individual legislators, urging support for the canal bill. In early June, Delegate Jones circulated his own pro-canal memorial, and on June 18, President Martin Van Buren signed the measure into law. Barely two years old, the Wisconsin Territory received its first substantial government land grant, a tract amounting to 139,190 acres. Byron Kilbourn could well be pleased with himself. He was sure completion of the canal was only a matter of time

Kilbourn's sense of pleasure at the time is revealed in a June 13 letter he wrote to Williams: "I am gratified with this result, and not less so with the praise you award to my exertions. – You need not be afraid of exciting my vanity, for I feel conscious of having executed what few would have undertaken, and still fewer could have succeeded in. But it is not in the Canal bill alone that I feel I have been useful. The division of the lands, the road appropriations and many other important measures are ... [attributed] largely to my exertions.... [I feel] fully compensated in the reflection that I have been of some service to the country, gratified my friends, and above all served my own best interests."[30] We would have difficulty finding a clearer statement of the entrepreneurial ethic of the day. Few people questioned the possible incompatibility of public service and private gain, especially in frontier Wisconsin.

Byron Kilbourn was euphoric, but there were some clouds on the horizon. Because Congress had set the price of canal lands at twice the regular rate, land-hungry settlers, short on cash, were sure to resent this provision. Congress had also refused to supply preemptive rights to squatters, so a settler had no guarantee that his claim might not be purchased by someone else. Thus were sown the seeds of future discontent. Timing also constituted a problem. The Panic of 1837 severely reduced the demand for western land because almost no one had specie to pay for it. Migration dwindled, with the result that land sales were less than anticipated. Generous payment provisions, designed to lure buyers, meant that only a fraction of the purchase price was actually paid into company coffers, resulting in less revenue for construction costs than anticipated. A major internal improvement project which at first appeared to be a sure thing suddenly seemed plagued with obstacles.

Standing in the wings were rival speculators, James Doty and Morgan Martin. For over two hundred years, the pathway through Wisconsin taken by Indians, traders, and missionaries alike was the Fox-Wisconsin route, running diagonally across the state from Green Bay to Prairie du Chien. In fact, these two important rivers were only a quarter mile apart at Portage. Were they connected, and the entire water route made navigable, Green Bay rather than Milwaukee would become the commercial center of the new territory. Morgan Martin was committed to the Fox-Wisconsin route, and he, like Kilbourn, one day received congressional support. His cousin, Judge Doty, had different plans for development, which he was sure to advance whenever the opportunity arose.

Undaunted, the canal board of directors appointed Kilbourn its "acting director" on September 27, 1838. In this capacity, he was authorized to employ workers, secure equipment, direct engineers in locating the final canal route, and oversee field operations. Identified as the project's chief backer at first, Kilbourn now became its very embodiment, and the phrase "Kilbourn's canal" came into general use. Governor Dodge told the legislature that canal completion was vital to the interests of the territory. But he was sensitive to the allegations that greedy speculators might take advantage of the situation, so he prohibited company personnel from purchasing lands along the canal's right of way. His motive was to discourage speculation; in the process, he discouraged a host of potential buyers, an additional deterrent to the already sluggish market for canal lands.

In spite of widespread verbal support, funds for construction remained insufficient. A new approach was necessary, and so on February 26, 1839, the legislature amended the canal law to allow territorial bonds to be sold to private investors. The lawmakers stipulated that these bonds must be *sold at par value*; they could not be discounted by several percentage points to attract prospective buyers, a practice common in eastern markets. Governor Dodge appointed John Tweedy, Kilbourn's own attorney, to serve as loan agent. Tweedy was a newcomer from Vermont trained at Yale. He was told to negotiate a $50,000 loan. Dodge also appointed four Milwaukeeans to represent *territorial* interests in the project. The impression that the canal was important primarily to Milwaukee began to gain currency.

In April of 1839, Kilbourn and Lapham were again in the field, this time laying out the final canal route. On July Fourth, an elaborate ceremony was staged at Milwaukee to celebrate the actual start of construction. As company president, Byron was toasted as "The settlers [sic] friend – Our claims made fast – our hearts made glad – our canal in successful commencement. In all this we see the finger of his handiwork." Another speaker celebrated "The Territory of Wisconsin, A fair and fruitful mother, may her children increase in prosperity as they increase in number, and may all their various interests be combined into one harmonious whole through the persevering enterprise of her

John Tweedy, Byron Kilbourn's attorney and later opponent.

most faithful and promising son, Byron Kilbourn." A third toast was even more laudatory of Kilbourn's efforts: "With head to conceive, heart to dare, and hand to execute, while he is at the helm, all is safe."[31]

But all was not safe, as soon became apparent.

As noted earlier, the main barrier to the construction of the canal was lack of money. There simply were insufficient funds in the territory to finance a project of this size. A state historian explained: "Income from stock subscription and land sales was altogether inadequate; by law the purchaser of either company stock or land was required to make only a 10 per cent down payment. The enthusiasm which accompanied the land sales of July 2, 3 and 5, 1839, resulting in the sale of 43,587 acres of land, grossed the company only $12,377.29, an amount much too small to meet even the costs of surveying the canal route."[32]

If the waterway were to be built, the money had to come from eastern capitalists. The legislature, Democratic at the time and friendly to the canal project, authorized a $50,000 loan based on the sale of territorial bonds. The plan was to secure some immediate cash to begin construction and rely upon future land sales to carry the rest of the load. But there was no market for securities which bore six percent interest. As John Tweedy told the governor, "Stocks of every nature [at New York City] were depressed to a lower point than they had at any time been for many years, not accepting [sic] the panic of 1837. The seven percent stock of New York City was selling at 95 [i.e. a 5 percent discount].... Money was commanding three times the ordinary interest in all the larger cities, and in smaller places of business."[33] Tweedy's observation is noteworthy given the fact that the legislature specifically stipulated that its territorial bonds must be sold at par value.

So the lawmakers tried again, this time approving a new bond issue of $100,000 (twice the earlier amount) at seven percent interest. The governor appointed a new loan agent, none other than Byron Kilbourn. Dodge probably figured that if anyone could secure funding, it would be Kilbourn, for he personally had more at stake than anyone else. On May 13, 1841, the governor officially authorized Kilbourn to find buyers for the new set of canal bonds. Faced with the need for a large sum of money, Kilbourn turned to Micajah Williams for help. Williams himself was not in a position to buy, but he had many wealthy friends, both in Ohio and in New York, who might be. It was to them that Kilbourn directed his appeals.

His first act was to purchase a thousand-dollar bond in his own name, depositing his money in Williams' Ohio Life Insurance and Trust Company. Then, he forwarded Ohio bank notes to John Tweedy, now canal receiver. Despite the fact that the Ohio notes were worth only 90 to 95 percent of face value, Tweedy accepted them in order to pay canal contractors. Apparently, Byron's aim was to establish a precedent and public faith in the canal project. Next, Kilbourn entered into an agreement with George Reed of Cincinnati for the sale of thirty canal bonds, depositing the bond certificates *without payment beforehand* in Williams' company. But Williams' firm was not a repository authorized by the Wisconsin legislature. Consequently, on July 16, 1841, Tweedy notified Williams that this arrangement was unacceptable.

Meanwhile, Kilbourn moved on to New York City. A new buyer, S. Higginbotham by name, agreed to take $25,000 of the territorial bonds, *provided four years of interest* was paid in advance and the proceeds of canal land sales were used to pay off the principal. But Governor Dodge rejected this because canal receiver John Tweedy refused to pay any interest whatever in advance. Dodge took the position that "Tweedy could place his own construction on the laws that were to govern him." Kilbourn then sold five shares to Colonel William Doughty, depositing the proceeds in his personal account. He sold another five shares in Albany, and again pocketed the money, in violation of his instructions. Neither of these two sales were reported to Tweedy, and no funds were forwarded to him. Another $15,000 of bonds were deposited at the bank of Vernon, in New York. This, too, was a violation of legislative instructions, since this bank, like Williams', did not meet legislative requirements. Driven by his desire to see his canal built as quickly as possible, Byron cut corners in the interests of securing the necessary backing.

The territorial legislature decided to investigate. Lawmakers were worried about the possibility of being saddled with a large debt. A select committee, composed mainly of Whigs and anti-canal Democrats, took a firm stand against the project, maintaining that both Dodge and Kilbourn exceeded their powers. They did so on these grounds: George Reed's bonds were issued without deposit; unauthorized banks were used as "legal agents;" and Kilbourn used his own discretion in negotiating canal loans. For these reasons the committee held that 55 shares of $1,000 each were "illegally and fraudulently disposed of and that the Territory is not liable for their redemption." Kilbourn's counter-argument maintained that his arrangement was the best possible under current economic conditions. Nonetheless, his negotiations were discredited. Although he eventually found buyers for his entire bond issue, he did so in violation of legislative instructions, with the result that canal funding was in doubt. A fatal blow to the canal project occurred in September 1841, when the newly appointed territorial governor, James Doty, revoked Byron's authority to sell canal bonds.[34] Doty had canal plans of his own, and they did not include Byron Kilbourn or Milwaukee.

Canal sentiment within the territory had changed markedly since the joyous celebration at Milwaukee two years earlier. Formidable opposition had developed, led by Kilbourn's Milwaukee rival, Alanson Sweet, Harrison Reed of the *Sentinel*, and James Doty. These three claimed they were concerned about settlers' rights, particularly the lack of a preemption clause in the canal law. They also stressed the high price of canal land. They did not mention their own private agendas, of course. When Kilbourn returned from a trip to Ohio in late July, he "found the whole country in a perfect ferment on this subject." "Vials of wrath," he wrote Williams, descended "in copious volume" on his head, and "denunciation of the whole community with here and there a few exceptions, in the madness of the moment was hurled unsparingly against me as an enemy to the settlers, and an ally of the speculators & c – But our enemies mistook their game, and before I had been home two weeks, they found they had mounted the wrong pony to ride over so rough a road. I turned out a <u>Stump Orator!</u> told the people the truth as to the passage of the bill and explained its provisions to their satisfaction."[35]

Perhaps Kilbourn's immediate listeners were satisfied, but Harrison Reed was not; he kept the fires of opposition burning steadily for the next year and a half in the pages of his newspaper. The *Sentinel* and the *Milwaukee Advertiser* engaged in a partisan battle of charge and counter-charge, which provided little new insight to readers but sold newspapers and perpetuated doubts about the canal, the canal company, and Byron Kilbourn in particular. Had canal funding been forthcoming, opposition would have faded quickly. Without it, opposition grew.

Governor Doty had reasons of his own for opposing Kilbourn and the canal. Foremost among these were his own plans for alternative canal routes. With extensive holdings at Green Bay, Fond du Lac, and Madison, Doty dreamed of a system of canals which would enhance the value of *his* holdings while bypassing Milwaukee entirely. Doty disliked Kilbourn personally, in part, perhaps, because he recognized the aggressive Milwaukeean as a formidable rival.

Kilbourn and Doty faced one another in the 1839 election for territorial delegate to Congress. Doty campaigned extensively on horseback, using his considerable charm to win votes. In contrast, Kilbourn and his new bride set out in a handsome carriage to seek support. He also published a lengthy statement of the internal improvement programs he favored. He carried Iowa and Green counties, but lost elsewhere in the territory.[36] George Jones, the territorial delegate who ardently supported the canal, was also defeated by the "Anti-Canal Party."

Other factors contributed to the defeat of the canal. One historian described the canal company as "hastily conceived" and "poorly managed." Directors were divided amongst themselves as to the proper route the canal should take, and the legislature was finally forced to step in and make a decision.[37] Milwaukee's east siders thought the canal would benefit only the west side of town, a legacy of the old rivalry between Juneautown and Kilbourntown. Outstate, voters felt Milwaukee alone would benefit from the canal; after all, its principal backers all came from there. Nationally, railroads were starting to be viewed as the transportation mode of the future. Once built, they could function in any season of the year, deliver passengers and freight faster than canal boats, and operate on a regular schedule. In support of this alternative mode of travel, Harrison Reed published a series of pro-railroad letters, the "anonymous" work of a New York speculator by the name of Paraclete Potter. Potter hoped to profit from Wisconsin projects for internal improvement in which he had an interest.[38]

Identified in the public mind with the unbuilt canal, Byron Kilbourn was often viewed with skepticism. Many thought of him as belligerent, overbearing, manipulative, aristocratic, and self-seeking. While Milwaukeeans supported him because they felt he had their best interests in mind, out-staters distrusted his motives and his eastern connections. They might admit that he got things done, but he seemed unconcerned about the means he employed, and never was as popular as Juneau, Walker, or Doty.

The original canal bill of 1838 stipulated that the canal company had ten years in which to complete construction. As a result, the canal question appeared on the legislative agenda of Wisconsin every year throughout the territorial period. Even though completion of the project no longer seemed likely, Kilbourn's land grant attracted the interest and hopes of many, especially those who dreamed of their own transportation projects.

Since funding was not forthcoming one might assume Kilbourn's canal was a complete failure, but such was not the case. In early April of 1841, contractor John Anderson began construction of a dam across the Milwaukee River. Located a mile and a quarter north of the settled part of town, the new structure was deemed "one of the most splendid artificial hydraulic powers in North America ... 480 feet long, eighteen feet deep and eighty-five feet wide. It took 4,000 cords of wood and 100,000 yards of gravel" to construct.[39] At the end of the dam, "nearest the westward of the town, there is a lock or feeder, eighty-seven feet long by fifteen feet wide, which supplies the hydraulic canal with any quantity of water required. This conductor extends to within a few yards of the town." It is located where Commerce Street now stands. A steady source of water power was essential if new industry were to be established in Milwaukee, and Kilbourn's canal section admirably met this need. Byron was co-founder of a hydraulic company, established in 1839. Having purchased water power rights from the canal company, the hydraulic firm could count on a steady income from mill owners for the foreseeable future.

By the year 1849, twenty-five canal-related companies were in operation, employing 250 people. The new industries did business worth $250,000 annually, supplying critical employment for scores of German immigrants. In 1850, Kilbourn established his own flouring mill a block from his house.[40] At the foot of Chestnut Street, "a 50,000 bushel grain elevator was built, said to be the 'largest in the world.'" In the decade before the Civil War, the grain trade flourished, with shipments going not only all over the Great Lakes, but overseas as well. By 1862, Milwaukee became "the greatest primary wheat market of the world," and the profits from the Kilbourn mill grew accordingly.[41]

While Byron Kilbourn personally lost $30,000 on the canal project, he at least had the satisfaction of knowing that his idea was sound. At the time, no one argued that canals were outdated, or that his canal could not be built. After all, the Erie Canal, created barely a decade earlier, was an unparalleled success. And rival Chicago chartered its "Illinois and Michigan Canal" in 1834, a project formally opened in 1848 and still in use today.

The Fox-Wisconsin waterway project championed by Morgan Martin proved equally disappointing. Although this historic route, traveled originally by birch-bark canoes, was made navigable to steam vessels by the mid-fifties, Martin spent a fortune on the project and went broke in the process. New Yorkers replaced Wisconsinites as the controlling faction in the company at the very time railroads spelled the end of the canal era in the state.[42]

By January of 1842, Increase Lapham was telling his brother that Kilbourn's canal project was about to be replaced by a railroad. Micajah Williams' original idea was about to have its day, or so Lapham thought. Even Governor Doty was on record as favoring a rail line between Milwaukee and the Mississippi.[43] Soon everyone wanted to get on the railroad bandwagon, but no rails would be laid for some time.

Kilbourn was not pleased and continued to seek the recovery of his personal investment in the canal until the Civil War. Even though Governor Doty terminated his canal project, Kilbourn sought and received Doty's support in his later efforts to win a land grant for the La Crosse and Milwaukee Railroad. Kilbourn returned the remaining canal bonds to Governor Doty early in 1843, whereupon the governor recommended cancellation of the entire offering. The legislature agreed. All sale of canal lands was halted by territorial law on March 27. Nevertheless, the canal died a slow death. In January of 1846, Henry Dodge, once again territorial governor, urged that preemption apply to settlers on canal lands and that Congress extend the time for sales. By December 31, 1847, canal expenses totaled $56,745. As a result, contrary to federal law, the remaining proceeds from the sale of canal lands were diverted to defray expenses of Wisconsin's two state constitutional conventions; unsold canal land was made part of the 500,000 acre grant to which each new state was entitled when it entered the union.[44]

Kilbourn's correspondence with Micajah Williams regarding the Rock River Canal makes clear that he was willing to go to great lengths to achieve success. In May of 1838, he asked Williams to lend him $300 so he could lobby eastern businessmen to buy canal stock. Concerned that Increase Lapham might be unknown in the east, he asked Williams to write a letter of endorsement "to give due weight" to Lapham's canal estimates. In August, Byron told Williams that he intended to run for the territorial council, as "much depends on getting proper action of the Legislature at the next session." In like fashion, a generation earlier, James Kilbourn had run for the Ohio Assembly to secure support for Sandusky as the northern terminus of the Ohio Canal.

So identified with the canal project had Byron become that we are not surprised to encounter his assertion, in September, that "I have the whole power of the canal measure in my hands."[45]

Profit motivated Kilbourn and Williams, profit they would receive from their sale of land. In December of 1838, Byron recommended that they withhold their lots from the market until the eastern terminus of the canal was determined, as this decision would enhance land values. In order to devote his entire attention to canal business, Kilbourn asked Williams for a $10,000 loan to clear up his personal debts – $3,500 to complete Leland's tavern, $2,500 for the steamship *Badger*, and $3,000 for Hinman's ice house. Once free of these obligations, Byron promised he would never again borrow money "not for the best friend in the world, or nearest kinsman." If he could relieve himself of his personal debts, he "could accomplish the desired end" and put the canal into successful operation, and so give an impetus to business which would place the partners in "the scale of importance to which our natural advantages entitle us."[46]

That Williams concurred in the importance Byron attached to his canal efforts is made clear by an undated document in his handwriting among his papers. The document is a proposal that the Franklin Bank of Columbus lend Kilbourn up to $50,000 to pay contractors and laborers on the Milwaukee and Rock River Canal. The bank's security was to be 6 percent Wisconsin territorial bonds, plus a mortgage on Byron Kilbourn's Milwaukee lots.[47]

Opposition to Byron's dream of a Milwaukee-Mississippi waterway remained strong in the rival communities of Green Bay and Racine, and in some cases in Milwaukee itself. Byron told Williams that the territory was filled with falsehood and misinformation, propagated by Sweet, Reed & Company, and "mobs, tar and feathers promised to me in copious quantities." To counteract these "falsehoods," he traveled through the territory giving speeches, and with the aid "of a few active friends defeated our enemies and sustained our measures."[48]

The first canal section put under contract was that "embracing the water power" at Milwaukee, the theory being that this canal link once completed would provide an immediate income. Suspicious of Kilbourn's preoccupation with Milwaukee, legislators insisted that 25 percent of a proposed canal loan be spent at the *western* terminus on the Rock River.

Byron remained confident of ultimate success until the fall of 1841 when, despite his strongest efforts, his arch rival, James Doty, was appointed governor of the territory. Kilbourn told Williams he had lost the earlier race for territorial delegate to Doty because "I undertook to be honest, and promulgated my real sentiments in relation to local improvements which you know would run counter to the wishes of many, who of course would oppose me strenuously ... while those whose wishes coincided with my views, found also that Doty coincided with theirs. He is professedly in favour of everything that anybody else is in favour of, and consequently was strongly supported by those who had no hopes from me, and [divided] those with me, whose views and wishes were the same as mine. In other words he can beat me at lying...." [49]

Convinced that his Rock River Canal would make Milwaukee the first city on the northern lakes, Kilbourn opposed anyone who stood in his way, especially the wily, powerful Doty. He labeled Doty a "vile knave," whose appointment to the governorship must be rejected "at all events, unless we agree to see misrule run rampant in Wisconsin for the next three years." In July of 1841, Kilbourn traveled east to Washington, D.C., specifically for the purpose of testifying against Doty before a Senate committee. He begged Micajah Williams to tell his presidential friend, William Henry Harrison, that he, Williams, would accept appointment as territorial governor, but all to no avail. President Harrison died a month after taking office, and his successor, John Tyler, appointed Doty as chief magistrate. [50]

On February 4, 1842, the canal fight was over for all practical purposes, though final settlement would take another six years.

Byron continued to seek repayment on his investment in canal stock into the 1860s but without success.

It was at this point that Kilbourn shifted his sights to a new goal – *a trans-Wisconsin railway system*. "The prospect at Madison," Increase Lapham wrote Williams, "is that the canal will be abandoned, the company paid off and discharged (not however without their own consent) and a new company formed to construct a Rail road to the Mississippi." The plan was to ask Congress to apply the canal grant to the railroad, and to make further donations in exchange for free mail. Even though Governor Doty himself endorsed this plan, the legislature refused to support it, and there the matter remained until the prospect of a statehood land grant arose six years later.

Byron Kilbourn had done everything in his power to build a canal between Milwaukee and the Rock River, a distance of under sixty miles. He had surveyed the prospective route at his own expense, described the canal's potential benefits in a series of carefully composed newspaper essays, and lobbied successfully for a congressional land grant, the first in Wisconsin history. Funding was the key to success but it was here that Kilbourn had failed in his purpose; he had been unable to secure needed eastern capital in a manner acceptable to the legislature.

Kilbourn did order construction of a dam on the Milwaukee River in 1841, and he authorized the building of a short canal section within a mile and a half of his house. It was these two improvements, however controversial elsewhere in the state, that guaranteed the city a head start in industrial development. The arrival of hard-working German immigrants provided an essential work force. In the antebellum era, a host of products were being produced in Milwaukee, ranging from iron, grain, and leather goods to cigars, furniture, and clothing. Byron's overall canal plan had failed, but that portion of the work completed in Milwaukee was an unqualified success – a result for which he could rightly take credit.

Kilbourn had invested $30,000 of his own money in the canal project. In the end, he lost all of this, but he more than made it up through the sale of land to German settlers, the establishment of his own grain mill beside the canal, the sale of water rights to incoming manufacturers, and the warehousing of grain and iron ore for export. Diversity of investment typified his financial decisions in the 1840s, fifties, and sixties.

The canal venture made Kilbourn's name a household word throughout the territory. Some viewed him as a smooth-talking easterner out to make a quick profit, while others, particularly his Milwaukee supporters, saw him as a man of action dedicated to making their city great.

The canal question came up each year before the territorial legislature, and was not finally put to rest until statehood in 1848.

Byron Kilbourn's limited ability to work with others – a shortcoming recognized earlier by Micajah Williams – played a decisive role in the failure of the project. He never learned how to court others for support, and he seemed to be incapable of delegating responsibility. Instead, he relied upon his own powerful will, energy, and ability. He simply did not understand how politics could ease his way. Politicians, he thought, were a necessary evil to cope with as best he could. Even his granddaughter was brought up to believe her illustrious ancestor was a "statesman," never a "politician."[51]

In Byron Kilbourn's day, as in our own, there was a thin line drawn between public interest and private gain. Let us turn next to this important difference.

Endnotes

[1] MPL, Comstock Papers. The authors are indebted to Orval Liljequist, former Head Librarian for Humanities, for calling this document to their attention. This description of the *Michigan* is based on Kilbourn's comments and information supplied by Paul Woehrmann, Librarian-in-Charge of the Great Lakes Marine Historical Collection of MPL.

[2] James Kilbourn to Whitfield Cowles, June 30, 1837, Cowles Family Papers.

[3] Increase Lapham to Darius Lapham, February 25, 1837, MCHS, Lapham Papers, Box 4, Folder 6.

[4] J. S. Buck, *Pioneer History*, p. 81.

[5] Jesse M. Van Slyck, *1854-55 Col. Van Slyck's Milwaukee City Directory, and Business Advertiser, Containing a Sketch of the Rise and Progress of the City of Milwaukee, an Alphabetical List of its Householders and Streets, Commercial and Business Men, with United States, State, County and City Officers, an Abstract of the New Banking Law, and Numerous Statistics Relating to the City, and Tables of General Interest, Established with a New Map of the City* (Milwaukee, Wis. Starrs' Book and Job Office, 1854), p. 9.

[6] Ewig, "Martin's Business Career," p. 56.

[7] In the days immediately after the circular was issued, Kilbourn refrained from issuing suits for non-payment. Byron Kilbourn to Micajah Williams, May 27, 1837, OHC, Williams Papers, Microfilm 96.

[8] Letter to Seneca Lapham, October 15, 1836, SHSW, Lapham Papers, Box 18.

[9] B. H. Edgerton to his father, cited in Graham P. Hawks, *Increase Lapham: Wisconsin's First Scientist*, published Ph.D. dissertation. University of Wisconsin-Madison, 1960, p. 43.

[10] Byron Kilbourn to Cicero Comstock, July 7, 1837, MPL, Comstock Papers.

[11] Ray A. Sueflow, *A Plan for Survival* (New York: Greenwich Publishing Company, 1965), p. 19.

[12] Theodore Mueller, "Milwaukee's German Cultural Heritage," *Milwaukee History* (Autumn 1987), p. 96.

[13] Robert W. Wells, *This is Kilbourntown* (Milwaukee: Renaissance Books, 1970), pp. 22-23.

[14] Paul Woehrmann, "Milwaukee German Immigrant Values: An Essay," *Milwaukee History* (Autumn 1987), p. 79.

[15] Still, *Milwaukee*, p. 72.

[16] Kathleen Conzen, *Immigrant Milwaukee, 1836-1860* (Cambridge: Harvard University Press, 1976), p. 144. John Kerler, Jr., told his countryman August

Frank that he preferred Wisconsin to Michigan because "my father was mainly looking for a place where Germans had settled and where one could manage better with his own language ... Milwaukee is first among the places partly inhabited by Germans.... [It] is the only place in which I found that Americans concern themselves with learning German, and where the German language and German ways are bold enough to take a foothold. You will find inns, beer cellars, and billiard and bowling alleys, as well as German beer something you do not find much of in this country," Harry H. Anderson, editor, *German-American Pioneers in Wisconsin and Michigan: The Frank-Kerler Letters, 1849-1864* (Milwaukee: Milwaukee County Historical Society, 1971), pp. 76-77.

[17] *Milwaukee Sentinel*. January 13, 1845; Conzen, *Immigrant Milwaukee*, p. 213; "Old Stocks and New Bonds," unpublished manuscript, MCHS, pp. 4-5; Koss, *Milwaukee*, pp. 156-157. Carl H. Knoche outlines Dr. Huebschmann's political career in the *Historical Messenger* vols. 27-28 (1972), pp. 114-131.

[18] Cited in Richard Zeitlin, *Germans in Wisconsin* (Madison: State Historical Society of Wisconsin, 1977), p. 8.

[19] Koss, *Milwaukee*, pp. 30, 36-37.

[20] Increase Lapham to Darius Lapham, February 25 and August 8, 1837, MCHS, Lapham Papers.

[21] G. Berquist, "Milwaukee's Byron Kilbourn," *Milwaukee History* (Spring 1993), p. 10.

[22] William R. Smith, *History of Wisconsin*, Part II: Documentary (Madison, Wis.: Beriah Brown, 1854), p. 355. Smith's *History* was compiled at the direction of the Wisconsin legislature and contains a historical overview of the canal favorable to Kilbourn's point of view. See Byron Kilbourn to W. R. Smith, September 10, 1854, Detroit Public Library, Smith Papers.

[23] For a detailed report of canal developments, see Lapham's *Documentary History of the Milwaukee and Rock River Canal* (Milwaukee: *Milwaukee Advertiser*, 1840). As secretary of the canal company, Lapham was directed to assemble this account.

[24] Byron Kilbourn to Micajah Williams, November 5, 1837, OHC, Williams Papers.

[25] Byron Kilbourn to Micajah Williams, December 28, 1837, OHC, Williams Papers.

[26] This analysis is based on several sources: Koss, *Milwaukee*, pp. 85-87; *History of Milwaukee, Wisconsin*. II, 1196; Alice Smith, *Doty*, p. 68. An examination of the whole canal dispute appears in Barnum, "The Politics of Public Aid," pp. 10-12. Byron Kilbourn's explanation as to why the canal failed appears in Buttles's diary, OHC, entry of June 26, 1843. For the battle

between Kilbourn and Sweet see the pages of the *Milwaukee Advertiser* and the *Milwaukee Sentinel*, especially the *Advertiser* for March 25, 1837, August 4 and September 1, 1838, and February 2, 1839, and the *Sentinel* of July 31, 1838 and September 15, 1840.

[27] Byron Kilbourn to Micajah Williams, December 28, 1837, OHC, Williams Papers.

[28] OHC, Williams Papers.

[29] Glorianna (Cowles) Matthews to W. Cowles, May 19, 1838, Cowles Family Papers.

[30] Byron Kilbourn to Micajah Williams, June 13, 1838, OHC, Williams Papers;

[31] *Milwaukee Advertiser*, July 6, 1839.

[32] A. Smith, *History of Wisconsin*, I, 452.

[33] J. H. Tweedy to Governor Henry Dodge, October 8, 1839, SHSW, Tweedy Papers.

[34] Kilbourn's negotiations to secure canal funding are described at length in Barnum, "Public Aid," pp. 18-27.

[35] Byron Kilbourn to Micajah Williams, September 19, 1838, OHC, Williams Papers.

[36] Wisconsin Territorial Papers, XXVII, 205.

[37] A. Smith, *History,* I, 451-452.

[38] *Ibid.*, 453.

[39] *History of Milwaukee Wisconsin*, p. 1173.

[40] W. Smith, *History*, II, 1173. Kilbourn's flour "sold at top prices in the Buffalo market." Margaret Walsh, *The Manufacturing Frontier: Pioneer Industry in Antebellum Wisconsin, 1830-1860.* (Madison: State Historical Society of Wisconsin, 1972), p. 181. Amos Sawyer initially ran the mill for Kilbourn and later purchased it in 1870.

[41] James S. Buck, *Milwaukee Under the Charter From 1854 to 1860 Inclusive* (Milwaukee: Swain & Tate, 1890), IV, 340. Economic historian Frederick Merk notes that "in 1860 the gristmill product sold for twelve times as much as any other commodity except sawed lumber." *Economic History of Wisconsin During the Civil War Decade* (Madison: State Historical Society of Wisconsin, 1916), p. 129. For an excellent analysis of the grain market in Wisconsin see John G. Thompson, "The Rise and Decline of the Wheat Growing Industry in Wisconsin" *Bulletin of the University of Wisconsin*, no. 292, Economic and Political Science Series, 5:3 (Madison: University of Wisconsin, 1909), 295-544.

[42] Ewig describes Martin's troubles in "Business Career," *passim.*

[43] Increase Lapham to Darius Lapham, January 20, February 4, 1842, MCHS, Lapham Papers; A. Smith, *History,* I, 352.

[44] W. Smith, *History of Wisconsin*, II, 432.

[45] Byron Kilbourn to Micajah Williams, September 16, 1839, OHC, Williams Papers.

[46] Byron Kilbourn to Micajah Williams, December 5, 1838, OHC, Williams Papers.

[47] OHC, Williams Papers, Microfilm 96, Roll 8, Box 8, Folder 4.

[48] Byron Kilbourn to Micajah Williams, September 16, 1839, OHC, Williams Papers.

[49] Byron Kilbourn to Micajah Williams, December 5, 1838, OHC, Williams Papers.

[50] Byron Kilbourn to Micajah Williams, February 24, July 20, 1841, OHC, Williams Papers.

[51] Maude K. Thorndike to the editor of the *Milwaukee Journal* September 7, 1945, MCHS, biographical clipping file, no. 88.

Public Good and Private Gain

Micajah Williams had been right all along. Byron Kilbourn was a competent surveyor and a conscientious canal engineer, capable of first-rate work in the field. But he had a blind spot. He had no sense of what it took to win widespread public support for a major project of internal improvement. In Ohio, Williams and Alfred Kelley had been Byron's mentors and overseers. They checked his work daily, double-checked every expenditure, paved the way for legislative support through diplomacy, and adeptly defended the project before the general public. The two commissioners from Cincinnati and Cleveland worked well together, on behalf of the general good, in an enterprise ripe with opportunity for corruption. In the end they triumphed, with their personal reputations intact.

Wisconsin was a different story. Here, in 1836, in a brand new territory, with a population of less than 25,000, Byron was on his own. There were no overseers, no fellow commissioners with whom to share responsibility. In the beginning, Byron was backed by a supportive governor and legislature. His efforts to build a canal to the Mississippi would succeed or fail largely because of what he did on his own. He was anxious to assume the mantle of leadership and determined to succeed.

Kilbourn seemed strangely indifferent to the possibility that his actions might bring harm or hard times to others. Once his mind was made up, criticism had little effect upon him. The end was what counted, he thought, not the means by which you achieved it. And, if your end was desirable, you should prevail.

At the close of the War of 1812, America found itself with a vast western territory to be developed. British forces vacated their posts in the northwest, to be replaced by American troops. A series of treaties with native tribes soon opened the way for new settlers. Young men in the east might feel their chance to get ahead was limited, but on the frontier, the sky was the limit. You could go as far as your talents would take you. Young men, without prospects, believed they could achieve success if they moved west, worked hard, and had a bit of luck.

There was, as one observer put it, an "almost universal *ambition to get forward."* He continued, "In England, once a journeyman weaver, always a journeyman weaver." But in America, half the men of wealth began as common day laborers.[1] (James Kilbourn, Byron's father, was a case in point.) "Broadening opportunities turned mobility into a scramble, as men previously satisfied with humble stations in life, became infected with the expectation of material gain."[2] Early Milwaukee was dominated by Yankee settlers who were especially energetic in their pursuit of gain. As Increase Lapham observed, "The people here are principally from New York and the states east of it. They all possess the enterprising go-ahead spirit of the New Englanders."[3] Unlike the countries of Europe, America was free of the threat of war, free to develop her enormous potential peacefully. Here was a land of opportunity where energetic white males could advance themselves on the basis of talent and hard work. Small wonder, then, that Americans simply turned their backs to the rest of the world and developed their own land.

The revolutionary world of Washington, Jefferson, and Adams was a world of culture and refinement, a world whose leaders admired European manners and ideas, a world of leisure and gentility for the wealthy not unlike the comfortable life enjoyed by an English country squire. But this was a world quite different from Jacksonian America. "No ambitious male in the early nineteenth century could have assumed, as the elite in Jefferson's generation did, that successful citizens took dinner in the early afternoon and allowed the balance of his day to personal cultivation and social pleasures."[4] The upwardly mobile entrepreneurs of Byron Kilbourn's youth valued work above all else. As an Englishman put it in the 1830s, "the American lives twice as long as others, for he does twice the work during the time that he lives.... He rises early, eats his meals with the rapacity of a wolf, and is the whole day about his business."[5] In such a society, respect was accorded the risk-takers. Practicality was the quality Americans most admired, not adherence to a class structure or a rigid code of conduct.[6] The Wisconsin Territory was, after all, part of the frontier. Its residents were like a body of teenagers, eager to strike out on their own, readily rejecting the values and lifestyles of their parents. The sharp trading practices of Yankee peddlers occasioned adverse comment but also grudging respect. In the race for advancement, shortcuts were condoned, and few seemed much concerned that all was not done strictly according to the rules. It was success in the end that mattered.

Byron Kilbourn was, as everyone agreed, a man of energy and determination. But he lacked moral discipline. From the age of six, he lived without the care and attention of a mother – the very person society assigned the task of teaching right from wrong. His father and older brother were usually away from home, so minimal guidance could be expected from them. He grew up amidst a bevy of adoring sisters who generally supported his every action. At an early age, he became determined to equal his father's accomplishments, and later, to surpass them.[7] The historical record suggests he was not particularly concerned about how he did so.

Furthermore, he was a man in a hurry. When he was thirty-three years old, he had a wife and two children to support, and no future prospects.[8] Until, that is, Micajah Williams opened the door of opportunity.

Territorial Wisconsin fit Kilbourn's temperament perfectly. The risks were high, but so were the rewards. Citizens looked the other way when Judge Doty bribed lawmakers with choice Madison lots in exchange for their votes on the location of the capitol.[9] Governor Barstow's supporters stuffed ballot boxes in an attempt to keep him in office. The newspapers were outraged but Barstow was forgiven, and went on to lead a regiment in the Union Army.[10] Newspaper editors accepted bribes in exchange for support of a candidate or a policy. These conditions, and others, led one historian to conclude that "the years 1854 to 1858 may claim to be the most unsavory in Wisconsin's political history." Everyone, it seemed, was out for No. 1. The prospect of instant wealth through quick land sales lured hordes of speculators to Milwaukee, as gold would later lure the fortune hunters of California.

Byron Kilbourn bet heavily on his canal and lost. But he did not lose his credibility in the process. Instead, his name became a household word throughout the territory. Many of his fellow Milwaukeeans concluded that what he had attempted, had been, after all, in their best interests, and that he was a daring advocate willing to take chances. They would forgive his later transgressions, when citizens elsewhere in the state would not.[11] Those who came to know him found him to be a man comfortable with large ideas, the sort of promoter you turn to when you want a big job done.

A newspaper reporter, evaluating the quality of three candidates for Congress in 1845, wrote the following:

> Byron Kilbourn is unquestionably a man of superior abilities, the characteristics of his mind being live-liness of perception, acuteness of understanding, searching penetration, indefatigable perseverance, and withal common sense. Never satisfied with any subject that occupies his attention till it is reduced to a demonstration, he is calculated to sift every word, thought, motive and action to the bottom.... These powers were propagated and extremely exercised by the practice of his profession of engineering; and it may be thought that his habits of severe thinking and of refraining from trivial conversation have rendered him less popular with the mass than others. He has even been accused of being aristocratic in his feelings; but we venture to affirm that if ever democracy found a genial habitation, it has found it in the breast of Byron Kilbourn ... he would as willingly shake the

The Bridge War of 1845 in which Byron Kilbourn played a key role.

hand of the farmer or mechanic, and grasp it as tightly too, as that of the first man in the nation. His whole soul is absorbed in the welfare of Wisconsin, and the breath of slander would fail to impeach his integrity; falsehood alone could successfully asperse his character. Suffice it to say, the distinction lies here – Upham or Darling would be the most successful candidates before the people; Kilbourn would be the most efficient representative on the floor of congress.[12]

When the territory was formally established in 1836, the voters of Milwaukee County elected Kilbourn to the legislature, but he chose not to serve.[13] Countless unfinished tasks demanded his attention at Kilbourntown. His place at the time, he believed, was in Milwaukee. It would be several years before he felt he could entrust his many business affairs to Increase Lapham in his absence.

What he did agree to do, in 1837, was to be a candidate for trustee for "Milwaukee west of the River." Upon election, his four fellow board members chose him to be their president.[14] At the time, Byron told Micajah Williams, he planned to run for territorial council in order to advance the cause of the canal.[15] But he did not actually do so, perhaps because of a late start and the heated opposition of Sweet and Reed.

In 1839, riding the crest of canal fever, Kilbourn decided to challenge incumbent James Doty for the strategic office of territorial delegate to Congress. Elected to succeed George Jones in September of 1838, Doty took office on January 3, 1839. Because of the separation of the Iowa territory from Wisconsin, a second election was scheduled for the following August. At the time the Democrats were the only political party in the territory. But as often happens in such cases, two factions within that party were constantly competing for control. The first of these was headed by Henry Dodge of Mineral Point, and it was pro-Van Buren and anti-bank. The second, led by James Doty of Green Bay, was anti-administration and pro-bank.

Governor Henry Dodge

Kilbourn was a supporter of Dodge, though he understood the importance banks could play in funding internal improvements.[16] Because of his domineering personality, Byron did not have a loyal support group of his own. Rather, he appealed to voters on the basis of their self-interest, and on his record of being able to get things done.

Removed from his judgeship by President Jackson, James Doty chose to remain a "nominal" Democrat, though he readily courted support from wherever he could get it. He was a man of knowledge and presence, long experienced in political matters, first at Detroit, then at Madison, and finally, in Washington. Doty had the ability to engage in "easy, familiar intercourse" with anyone he met. Suave and charming, he knew how to court voters, and his views seemed to agree with everyone else's. Moses Strong described him as "the most popular man in the territory."[17] Doty left nothing to chance; he made an exhaustive canvass of the electorate by horseback, the first such campaign Wisconsinites had seen. He was indeed a formidable opponent.

The foremost supporter of the Milwaukee and Rock River Canal, Byron Kilbourn appealed to three constituencies: those who hoped to profit from the canal, voters in Milwaukee and Jefferson counties along the canal route, and Dodge supporters in the lead region.[18] He campaigned in an expensive carriage, accompanied by servants and his new bride from the east. To many struggling settlers, he seemed the candidate of privilege, not one of them. Harrison Reed's hostile *Sentinel*, perhaps the most powerful newspaper in the territory at the time, ridiculed Kilbourn's campaign style: "Even he who is usually so stern, so repulsive and so forbidding in his manners, even *he*, it is said, has for a week relaxed his natural sternness and severity, and become wondrous polite to the 'dear people' whom he has heretofore treated so cavalierly and, with affectionate kindness, is seen to shake hands with 'Tom', and daily heard to ask about the health of 'Dick', and with almost melting tenderness, enquire after the health of 'Harry's wife and children.' But it all won't do. The sudden condescension of Mr. Kilbourn is <u>no go</u>." According to the *Sentinel*, "the honest, hard-working and independent settlers have visions too keen, and intellects too clear for the shallow devices of petty demagogues, who with Kilbourn at their head, seek to destroy Doty and triumph over the people. . . ."

Kilbourn lost the congressional race to Doty by a vote of 2,125 to 1,159. The entry of a third candidate into the field may have drawn some votes away from him, but he simply wasn't the campaigner Doty was.[19] At a time when everyone seemed to have a pet project of his own, Kilbourn may have been ill-advised to publish a long list of the internal improvements *he* favored. Another episode in the ongoing battle between Kilbourn and Doty occurred five months later when, Doty, as Wisconsin's territorial delegate, sought to wrest a lucrative federal publishing contract away from Kilbourn's *Advertiser* and give it to Harrison Reed's *Sentinel*.[20]

In 1840, William Henry Harrison won the presidential election, and as the nation's new chief executive, had the power to appoint Wisconsin's next territorial governor. Doty wanted the job, and Kilbourn was determined to do all in his power to prevent him from getting it. First, he sought to persuade his Virginia partner, William M. McCarty, to move to the territory and serve as governor. When this effort failed, he turned to Micajah Williams with the same proposal. Byron assumed Williams need only tell his Cincinnati friend, Harrison, of his interest, and the appointment would be forthcoming.[21] But fate intervened; Harrison died barely a month after assuming office, putting Doty's future in the hands of Vice President John Tyler and the U. S. Senate. Kilbourn and his allies failed to persuade the senators and the new president of Doty's unfitness for office, with the result that Byron's arch enemy was appointed. One of the new governor's first acts was to rescind Byron Kilbourn's authority to sell stock in the Milwaukee and Rock River Canal, thus bringing to a close Byron's dream of a waterway from Milwaukee to the Mississippi.

For several years, Byron occupied himself with local matters. In 1839, he and Solomon Juneau proposed the incorporation of a single "town of Milwaukee." The legislature promptly agreed, though the long-running rivalry between east and west side continued; both Kilbourntown and Juneautown exercised strict financial control over their own parts of town.

The cost of construction and maintenance of bridges over the Milwaukee River was a particularly thorny issue. Sectional feelings ran high. Both sides were convinced that the other was unwilling to pay its fair share. Early on, Byron opposed the construction of any bridge at all, as he wished to isolate his east side rivals as much as possible. But in 1844, in the midst of his campaign to become a member of the territorial legislature, he reversed himself. As often happens when a public figure changes his mind, voters were unsure of which view Kilbourn really favored.

There was no question about Kilbourn's leadership of the west side, however. Tempers flared when west siders destroyed the Chestnut Street bridge, the best then in existence in Milwaukee. This event marked the start of the so-called "bridge war" of 1845. Kilbourn's tall house by river became the target of east side artillery men, and east siders armed themselves, prepared to attack their neighbors. At the last minute, however, cooler heads prevailed. A popular orator of the day, J. E. Arnold, reminded listeners that Kilbourn's daughter, Glorianna, had died of consumption the day before, and that the family was now in mourning. Out of respect for the dead, he urged the angry citizens to disperse. Sheepishly they did.[22]

Kilbourn's second daughter, Lucy, died in Ohio the following November, so it was not until a year later that politics again occupied his attention.[23] The City of Milwaukee was formally established January 31, 1846, and the first city-wide election took place the following April. To no one's surprise, Solomon Juneau, Milwaukee's first permanent settler, was elected Mayor. Byron Kilbourn, leader of the west side, was chosen as one of three aldermen to represent the second ward.[24] In the following eight months, the Milwaukee board of aldermen – or Common Council as it became known – held sixty-three meetings; in fifty-five of these, Byron Kilbourn was an active participant. Juneau appointed him to the standing committees on finance and the judiciary, and he played a major role in the first year of the city's existence. Kilbourn offered the council's first motion, and shortly thereafter, Juneau asked him to help prepare a set of Council Rules and Regulations, and a city-wide Code of Ordinances. On May 21, Kilbourn refused election to serve as "acting mayor" in Juneau's absence; the role of temporary moderator held little appeal to this activist. Between April 10 and December 31, Byron proposed 123 motions which reveal much about his public and private interests: city appointees, printing of council procedures, street paving, the grading of sidewalks, license regulation, police and fire protection, bridge inspection, restriction of the "running at large of horses, cattle, hogs and geese," debt accumulation, prevention of gambling (this from one of the community's foremost land speculators!), instructions regarding contagious diseases, removal of harbor obstructions, care of the poor. Three motions seem especially noteworthy: the appointment of Kilbourn's friend and associate, Increase Lapham, as surveyor for wards 2, 4, and 5; Kilbourn's personal request for permission to build a river wharf in ward 2; and a directive that personal property taxes be spent only in the ward where they were raised (a reminder of earlier autonomy east, west, and south of the river).[25] Byron Kilbourn was a major player in city affairs, and would remain so for many years to come.

The movement to convert Wisconsin from a territory to a state began in 1839, when Governor Dodge recommended the measure in his annual address to the legislature. But no action resulted. Dodge's successor, James Doty, repeated the process, but on two separate occasions the proposal was rejected. Sectionalism, boundary disputes, the prospect of increased debt and higher taxes, and factional politics all played a part in preventing the change. Then on January 6, 1846, Morgan Martin, serving as territorial delegate to Congress, received permission to introduce an enabling act on the floor of Congress, a bill ultimately passed on August 6.

In January of 1847, Henry Dodge, once again territorial governor, again recommended statehood. This time voters endorsed the idea enthusiastically. On August l, the governor apportioned the territory for purposes of delegate selection, and on September 7, 125 delegates were selected. D. A. J. Upham of Milwaukee was chosen to preside. The constitutional convention was composed mainly of Democrats, with a few Whigs. But as we have seen, Wisconsin Democrats often disagreed with one another. The convention met for eleven weeks and two days (much too long, many voters thought), and completed its work on December 16.[26]

The proposed state constitution was a liberal document for its day, and was roughly modeled after that of the state of New York. Five provisions were particularly controversial:

1   Banks of any sort were prohibited (a reflection of the strong negative feelings held by a debtor society).
2   State judges were to be *elected* rather than appointed.
3   Property rights of women were to be protected.
4   The homesteads of debtors were to be exempt from creditors.
5   The question of Negro suffrage was to be settled in a special referendum.

The time period between December 16 and April 7 was one of great agitation. "Pro" and "anti" mass meetings were held throughout the state. Byron Kilbourn, who refused election to the first convention, spoke out against the proposed constitution, even though his second ward Germans were solidly behind it. As an advocate of internal improvements, Kilbourn was quite conscious of the crucial role banks could play in providing capital. Furthermore, he believed the state constitution was not the place to experiment with social change, such as women's rights and Negro suffrage; these matters, he believed, should be left to the later judgment of the legislature and the people. On this occasion, a majority of Wisconsin's voters agreed with him, and the document went down to resounding defeat.[27]

*Mayor Byron Kilbourn, painting by
Samuel Brookes, 1848.*

But local politicians had no intention of abandoning statehood, for they were anxious to be a part of the national election in 1848. So on September 27, the governor called for a special session of the legislature to meet on October 18. New ground rules were established for a new constitutional convention. This time, there were to be half as many delegates, 69 to be exact, and they would be urged to avoid controversial planks and conduct their business promptly when they came together on December 15. Morgan Martin, author of the enabling act, was made chairman. Byron Kilbourn was chosen as one of Milwaukee's seven representatives, along with the talented new editor of the *Milwaukee Sentinel*, Rufus King. Both men would play important roles in the six-week session.

One of Martin's first acts was to appoint Kilbourn to the fifteen-member standing committee on "general provisions." This blanket term was intended to cover a variety of matters: a preamble, state boundaries and the process of admission to the union, suffrage, internal improvements, taxation, finance and the public debt, militia, property rights and eminent domain, and a citizen's bill of rights, which ultimately would include twenty articles. Kilbourn was elected by his peers to head this important committee.

Among the first to speak in the new convention, Byron advocated economy of action. He suggested that members omit from their constitution the provisions that prevented acceptance of the earlier one, leaving such matters to the decision of the new state legislature. This approach, he said, would greatly reduce the length of their time together, and would thus be popular with the voters. While his fellow delegates did not follow his advice to the letter, they did buy his argument about the omission of controversial reforms. They also decided that their constitution should be an entirely new document, not a slightly altered version of the old. In addition to committee responsibilities, Kilbourn often addressed the assembly. He recommended a candidate for "messenger," and favored accepting the lowest bid for printing the proceedings. Sometimes he expedited meetings by moving adjournment when all essential business was completed. He opposed the recapture of fugitive slaves without evidence of ownership. He favored exempting "Negroes and mulattos" from service in the state militia. In contrast to nativist-oriented Whigs, Kilbourn favored full citizenship for foreigners after one year's residency, a position sure to be popular with Milwaukee's growing immigrant population. But he supported the Whigs on banking, and thought banks should be allowed in the new state, with the concurrence of the people. He also favored the use of the school fund for internal improvements, such as canals and railroads – a stand many others did not share.[28] Like most Democrats of his time, he combined compromise with traditionalism. Throughout the territory he was viewed quite differently; some thought of him as an underhanded turncoat because they had put funds into canal lands and that project failed; others saw him as Milwaukee's foremost promoter and progressive man of action. Few voters were neutral about him.

Two observers help us understand how Kilbourn was perceived. Rudolph Koss used the process of comparison to explain his thinking. He described Solomon Juneau and Byron Kilbourn as "two men differing in character and spiritual makeup." Juneau, Koss declared, "was an impulsive, brave and generous hearted Frenchman having none of those harsher characteristics usually associated with the business man." Kilbourn, on the other hand, "had a comprehensive mind, a strong willpower, and a head that knew how to gain his end, a firm unshakable makeup armed by nature to withstand attack. He was quick to fathom the mind of an adversary, never at a loss for an idea, and endowed with a store of worldly wisdom and vision." Both were honorable men, Koss concluded, one "guided by the letter of the law in worldly affairs, the other by the impulse of a great heart."[29]

Two sharply different pictures of Kilbourn, rendered several years apart, are provided by Henry Tenney, a journalist and lawyer who settled in Milwaukee in the 1840s. New to the city in 1847, he told his brother "Milwaukee politicians are no better than they are called. Kilbourn regards nothing but his own selfish ends. He wants 3 things: to get a banking system, to swindle the territory on the canal matter, and to go to the U.S. Senate."

Seven years later the same writer gives us an entirely different profile:

> I have rec'd a letter from Byron Kilbourn in wh. he announces his intention of being a candidate for US Senator and asks me to give him a lift, & I have replied that I would certainly do so. This I did, not because he asked it, but because I have long believed that he is one of the very best men for that post in the state. I do not know how you

may stand affected in the matter, but as I am really very desirous to see Mr. K. elected, I have thought it best to discuss a few of my opinions to you in the hope that you may also give him your support.

In the first place, it is a fact, & you will readily believe it, that there are very few Wisconsin politicians for whom I would wiggle a pen or lift a finger. I have seen too much of them. But Kilbourn is an exception for three reasons. He is a very able, sound man – one of the very largest in the state. We need such in the US Senate. Small potatoes may pass in other places, but if there are any men among us of real capacity we need them in the U.S. Senate. That body has been running down for years. I feel really a national interest & duty in seeing an able man elected. Kilbourn in my judgment is by far the ablest man spoken of. In fact, all the rest are utterly unfit. Doty, Farwell, Fred Horn, Barstow, etc. are not of the right mould. The only thing against Kilbourn is his supposed dishonesty. I do not think him a saint in that particular. Yet there is not one of the above, except Farwell that can compare with him in that respect. He is not dishonest in the ordinary sense of the word. He tells the truth, pays his debts, & performs all his engagements as honorably as any other businessman. In politics, canals, and railroads, etc, he certainly tried to carry his ends by the means best adapted to the purpose, but he is never treacherous or mean – even in these things he can always be depended on as true to his friends and engagements. More cannot reasonably be expected from a public man in Wisconsin....

I suppose the choice will be between Doty, Kilbourn & Farwell [the former governor]. It seems to me the choice is plain. Doty you never could go for. Farwell, clean person as he is, hasn't the brains – not 1/100 part – to face the empty seats of Clay, Webster, J. Q. Adams, & such men. Kilbourn is able to sit in the U.S. Senate with honor, & be useful to the state. If the anti-Barstow and anti-Doty influences will concentrate on him, he can be elected, & he is not one of those who forget their friends....[30]

The second time around, territorial voters approved the results of convention deliberations. Wisconsin's new constitution received a favorable vote of 74 percent to 41 percent for its predecessor. The referendum on Negro suffrage was voted on in the election of 1849; the ballots ran 5,256 for, 4,075 against. But the state election board ruled that this was not a true "majority" since 31,000 votes had been cast in the general election. Not until 1866 did Negro suffrage come to the state. One further development is worth noting. Delegates from both state conventions chose to finance their expenses by use of unspent canal funds – a sum amounting to $80,000. Ironically, Byron Kilbourn's canal, which opponents branded a failure, laid the basis for Milwaukee's industrial growth and funded two constitutional conventions.

A prominent participant in Wisconsin's second constitutional convention, Byron Kilbourn ran for mayor of Milwaukee in the spring of 1848. In a close contest, he defeated Whig candidate Rufus King by a vote of 1,079 to 881.[31] On April 12, Kilbourn delivered his inaugural address to the Common Council.[32] Not surprisingly, his major focus was upon internal improvements, and his program included better streets and sidewalks, a railroad to the Mississippi (no track had yet been laid in the state), plank roads, and the establishment of a new harbor entrance. Secondary consideration was given to police and fire protection and to public health.

Kilbourn's primary concern was the development of a "straight cut" to improve lake access to the inner harbor created by the confluence of the Milwaukee and Menominee Rivers. He pointed out that the people had already voted in favor of this improvement; the problem was, how to raise the necessary funds. Everyone hoped the federal government would pick up the tab and that the project would soon be completed. But in the end, the city funded most of the expense itself ($445,000 to $84,000), and the "cut" finally began functioning nine years later.[33]

The summer of 1848 found Kilbourn active in a quite different sphere, that of national politics. The preeminent question of the day involved the possible extension of slavery into the new states of the union. The majority Democratic Party was split down the middle. Southern Democrats approved, or at least tolerated, slavery. They wanted to preserve their traditional role in decision-making, and saw an increase in the number of slave states as a way to do so. Northern Democrats, on the other hand, opposed the extension of slavery – some more fervently than others.

Distrustful of the normal political process, a faction that wished to restrict slavery to its present domain formed a new political party. In August, a "Free Soil" convention was held in Buffalo, New York. Mayor Byron Kilbourn of Milwaukee was named one of the honorary vice presidents, and the delegates nominated former President Martin Van Buren as its candidate for the nation's highest office. In the election that followed, Wisconsin voters split their vote, awarding 38 percent to the Democratic candidate, Lewis Cass, 35 percent to the Whig, Zachary Taylor, and 27 percent to Van Buren.[34] Nationally, the splinter votes cast for Van Buren guaranteed Taylor's election.

Having been chosen mayor of the state's largest city, with a name well-known throughout the state, Byron hoped to be selected as one of Wisconsin's first U.S. Senators. But the two houses of the legislature meeting together decided otherwise. They cast a majority vote for former Governor Henry Dodge to represent the southwest, and Issac Walker, a conservative Milwaukee attorney and brother of George Walker, to represent the east. Old-line Democrats resented Kilbourn's recent desertion of the national party, and though he was acceptable to Wisconsin's

Whigs, he lost to Walker by a vote of 45 to 18.[35] As one historian put it, Byron Kilbourn was "perhaps the most commanding figure in the early politics of Milwaukee." Kilbourn, he said, "was not primarily a politician." His real motive for running for office was "to protect his material interests." Hence, the marriage between public good and private gain.

By 1849, Kilbourn had shifted his interest to railroads. While no one any longer disputed their superiority to canals and plank roads, everyone knew they were expensive to build. Once again, money was the problem. Who would provide the funds necessary? Kilbourn's solution was truly innovative: he persuaded the Milwaukee Common Council to accept farm mortgages in exchange for city bonds, which he could then market in the east. By May 1851, the council authorized $234,000 for railroad con-struction, and such funding continued to escalate in the years to come. While we will deal with the topic of railroads at length in the next chapter, it is notewor-thy that Byron relied upon his powers of persuasion to get the job done. As in the case of the Milwaukee and Rock River Canal, he was the project's foremost fund-raiser. His success in creating Wiscon-sin's first railroad in 1851 (a twenty-two-mile line from Milwaukee to

Sherman Booth, abolitionist editor of the Waukesha Freeman.

Waukesha) enhanced his credibility as a man of action, and in 1854 Milwaukee voters again elected him mayor. From that point on, the faction he represented controlled city politics for many years.[36]

The year 1854 was memorable for another reason. On March 20, a protest group at Ripon, Wisconsin, formed a new political organization, which they called "the Republican Party." On July 13, a mass meeting at Madison also adopted the name, and soon "Republican" clubs sprang up all over the north. Within two years of its founding, the Republican Party came to replace the Whigs as America's alternative to the Democrats.

Kilbourn decided to make a second run for the U.S. Senate in 1854. He went to abolitionist editor Sherman Booth seeking support. Booth remembered their conversation this way: "Mr. Booth, you said last winter if you had more money you would enlarge the size and scope of your paper. I want to be United States Senator, and I want the support of your paper, and if I can have it I will give you $5,000." Although Booth appreciated Kilbourn's earlier support of the Free Soil Party, he refused the offer, and did so a second time a year later. "It was common practice in Milwaukee's pioneer period to purchase men, or subsidize newspapers, and 'no odium' was attached to such efforts."[37]

Here lies the crux of the dilemma: it is bribery when a candidate for office offers money in exchange for support. But what is it if financial assistance is given to those who already intend to support the candidate? Is this also bribery? The use of money and gifts to gain favorable consideration from a client is, and has been, a widespread practice in business. Is it likewise permissible in politics? The historical record for Wisconsin in the 1850s is anything but clear on this point, as we shall see.

In February of 1855, Kilbourn became the senate candidate of the "regular Democrats." He went into the legislative election with a promised majority of nine votes, "but after several unsuccessful ballots" he lost the race to Charles Durkee of Kenosha by a single vote.[38]

Despite his inability to win a seat in the U.S. Senate, Kilbourn maintained an interest in politics. In 1859, he studied the national scene and concluded that the new Republican Party would probably win a clean sweep in the next election, for slavery had split the Democratic Party in two.[39] The Civil War broke out in the spring of 1861, only days after the election of the country's first Republican president. The momentous event had the effect of dividing the country along new political lines. Suddenly, there were unionists and secessionists, Peace Democrats, and War Democrats, copperheads and radical Republicans. For the duration of the war, President Lincoln led a "Union Party," whose doors were open to all who favored the continuation of the American republic. Byron Kilbourn aligned himself with the War Democrats. He had no sympathy for the peace-at-any-cost wing of his own party. The fact that his son was fighting in the Union Army undoubtedly strengthened his resolve.

The final political episode in Byron Kilbourn's career involved a letter he wrote to President Lincoln on September 1, 1864. At the time, the country had been at war for more than three years. Grant's siege of Richmond involved heavy casualties, as did Sherman's, at Atlanta. Such losses gave a temporary "impetus to the peace crusade." On August 29, the Democrats nominated General George McClellan as their candidate for president. Radical Republicans, aware that Lincoln did not favor the harsh peace they had in mind, chose John C. Fremont, who had been the Republican candidate in 1856. Everywhere there were rumors of a "conspiracy to establish a Northwest Confederacy." Kilbourn apparently thought Lincoln needed "sympathy and counsel." His letter is as follows:

> The peace men have held their convention at Chicago and adjourned. They have hurrahed loudly and made much noise. Be not dismayed but of good courage. The people of the U.S. will sustain

you and preserve the Union. The best argument for peace is to strengthen Grant & Sherman.

Your only fault has been, a little too weak in the back and too limber in the knees. Your enemies only give abuse for your lenity.

Please take a little stiffening and give them a few doses of what they falsely place to your account, viz., a stern exercise of power. Catch some of these American Knights [St. Louis conspirators] and hang them, and the peace men will give you credit for energy. A little Jacksonian treatment will make them good citizens.[40]

Once again, Byron demonstrated his firm belief in the "strong leader" approach. Unlike Mr. Lincoln, he did not face an uphill battle for re-election in wartime. Nor did he have to contend with a Union Party made up of a host of competing factions. Abraham Lincoln was a consummate politician.[41] For all his other talents, Byron Kilbourn would never merit this label.

The 1850s was the era of the steam locomotive in Wisconsin. Kilbourn led the way with his Milwaukee and Waukesha, followed by the Milwaukee and Mississippi, and the La Crosse and Milwaukee. It was this chapter in his life that ultimately resulted in his downfall as one of Wisconsin's most prominent citizens.

Endnotes

[1] George Rogers Taylor, *The Transportation Revolution, 1815-1860*, IV, *Economic History of the United States* (Armonk, N.Y.: M. E. Sharpe, Inc., 1951), 4.

[2] *The Rising Glory of America*, p. 10.

[3] Increase Lapham to Darius Lapham, February 25,1837, MCHS, Lapham Papers.

[4] Robert H. Wiebe, *The Opening of American Society* (New York: Alfred Knopf, 1984), p. 271.

[5] Ibid.

[6] Richard D. Heffner, "Introduction," *Alexis de Tocqueville, Democracy in America* (New York: Penguin Books, 1956), p. 18.

[7] Writing four years after James's death, Byron informed a Connecticut audience he did not intend to squander his fortune on "thankless efforts to promote the public interest" as his father had. Address to the Kilbourn Historical and Genealogical Society, SHSW microfiche.

[8] According to Wiebe, "young males ... had at most a decade and probably less to reveal their talents [to succeed]." *Opening*, p. 271.

[9] "The building of the territorial capitol," Milo Quaife wrote, "afforded a spectacle of greed, incapacity and chicanery on the part of the men to whom the trust was committed which should have at least wrought the permanent forfeiture of the confidence of their fellows; yet it seems in no wise to have affected the public career of Doty, the man who stood foremost among the offenders." Cited in *History of the Fox River Valley, Lake Winnebago and the Green Bay Region*, William A. Titus, ed. (Chicago: The S. J. Clarke Company, 1930), I, 335.

[10] Barstow organized the Third Wisconsin Regiment in 1862; one of his officers was Byron Kilbourn's son.

[11] Austin suggested that Kilbourn "had done so much in the building of the city that it seems he could do no wrong in the eyes of Milwaukeeans." *The Milwaukee Story*, p. 44.

[12] *Milwaukee Courier*, May 7, 1845, cited in *The United States Biographical Dictionary and Portrait Gallery of Eminent and Self-Made Men* (Chicago: Biography Publishing Company, 1877), p. 56.

[13] Koss, *Milwaukee*, p. 56.

[14] Barnum, "Public Aid," p. 6.

[15] July 16, 1838, OHC, Williams Papers.

[16] *Wisconsin in Three Centuries, 1834-1905* (New York: Century, 1906), II, 305-306.

[17] Kenneth M. Duckett, *Frontiersman of Fortune: Moses M. Strong of Mineral Point* (Madison: State Historical Society of Wisconsin, 1955), p. 39.

[18] The *Milwaukee Sentinel* referred to Kilbourn as "the great projector of the Canal," July 16, 1839.

[19] *Wisconsin Territorial Papers*, XXVII, 205.

[20] Kilbourn supplied space for the *Advertiser* printing office in the second floor of his Chestnut (Juneau) Street warehouse along with financial backing for the newspaper. *Milwaukee Advertiser*, October 20, 1836.

[21] Byron Kilbourn to Micajah Williams, February 24, 1841, OHC, Williams Papers.

[22] A full account of the "Bridge War" of 1845 appears in Koss, *Milwaukee,* pp. 197-209.

[23] Buttles' diary, entry of November 8, 1845. The *Milwaukee Sentinel* reported that Lucy was fifteen years old when she died on November 8. She was buried beside her mother in Worthington.

[24] Wheeler, *Chronicles*, p. 182.

[25] Milwaukee (Wis.) Board of Aldermen. Minutes, 1846-1874, MCHS, *passim*.

[26] See Milo M. Quaife, ed., Wisconsin Historical Publication, *The Convention of 1846, Collections*, Vol. XXVII, Constitutional Series, Vol. II (Madison: State Historical Society of Wisconsin, 1919).

[27] The actual vote taken April 6, 1847 was 14,116 for, 20,231 against. A. Smith, *History*, I, 665.

[28] Quaife also edited the proceedings of the second state constitutional convention. See Wisconsin Historical Publications, *The Attainment of Statehood, Collections*, Vol. XXIX, Constitutional Series, Vol. IV (Madison: State Historical Society of Wisconsin, 1928). Kilbourn spoke against the first constitution in March 1847. Milo M. Quaife, ed., *The Struggle Over Ratification, Collections*, Vol. XXVIII, Constitutional Series, Vol. III (Madison: State Historical Society of Wisconsin, 1920), 328, 519.

[29] *Milwaukee*, pp. 75-76.

[30] Henry Tenney to Horace Tenney, December 30, 1847, December 4, 18[55?], SHSW, Tenney Papers.

[31] Wheeler, *Chronicles*, p. 199.

[32] *Inaugural Address of Byron Kilbourn: Mayor of the City of Milwaukee* (Milwaukee 1848), MPL.

[33] Larson, *Financial History*.

[34] Koss, *Milwaukee*, pp. 268-269; A. Smith, *History*, 1, 638.

[35] Conard, *History of Milwaukee*, I, 101.

[36] Still, *Milwaukee*, p. 144.

[37] Julius Bleyer, "Unpublished History: Sherman M. Booth," *Once a Year* (1903), p. 9. See also *MCHS Newsletter*, October 1991, "A Historic Manuscript is Received."

[38] Conard, *History*, I, 22, 101.

[39] Duckett, *Strong*, p. 153. In the mid-1850s Kilbourn entertained a variety of political notables in his home, including Senator Stephen Douglas, later famous as Lincoln's opponent in the series of 1858 debates. James G. Brazell, "Byron Kilbourn's Home on Second Street," c. 1900, newspaper file, MCHS.

[40] Frank L. Klement, "Kilbourn Gives Advice to Lincoln," *Historical Messenger*, 23:1 (March 1967), 8.

[41] For an excellent account of the election of 1864 see John C. Waugh, *Reelecting Lincoln: The Battle for the 1864 Presidency* (New York: Crown Publishers, 1997).

Railroads, Land Grants and "Liberal Compensation"

The citizens of Milwaukee first issued a call for a railroad between their town and the Mississippi River at a mass meeting on September 17, 1836. Byron Kilbourn served as secretary for this gathering, the first of many railroad assemblies in which he participated. But this was not his first exposure to the idea of railroading. His imaginative grandfather, John Fitch, had created a model of a combination steamboat-locomotive, which the family found in the attic of James Kilbourn's Worthington home after his death in 1850.[1] We do not know whether Byron ever actually examined this device, but we do know that Byron's father, James, campaigned for a Columbus-Sandusky railroad in 1825, after he lost his battle to make Sandusky the northern terminus of the Ohio Canal.[2] As a family member and canal employee, Byron could hardly have been unaware of this effort. Micajah Williams, Byron's Cincinnati partner, conceived of visualizing a rail line from Lake Michigan to a navigable inland river in the spring of 1835.[3] No doubt Byron knew of this plan as well.

Increase Lapham, Kilbourn's business agent, told his Ohio relatives on August 17, 1836, that an application for a Milwaukee to Mississippi railroad was "soon to be made."[4] Kilbourn was sympathetic to such thinking, even before the proposal presented to his neighbors.

Governor Dodge, attentive to the needs of his Milwaukee constituents, recommended a trans-Wisconsin line to the territorial legislature at Belmont on October 26. But the new territory had no funds for internal improvements, so no action was taken. Everyone agreed railroads were superior to canals. This fact had already been demonstrated in Great Britain and on the East Coast. But everyone also knew that a railroad would cost a great deal more to build than a canal. Unable to finance such an undertaking on its own, Wisconsin turned to the federal government for help. Territorial Delegate George W. Jones asked for an appropriation to survey a rail route *from Milwaukee to San Francisco* in 1837. His petition "produced a great laugh and hurrah in the house," but no action was taken. Then in 1838, Congress voted $2,000 to survey a much shorter route, from Milwaukee to Dubuque, a project never completed.[5] Byron Kilbourn's less expensive Milwaukee and Rock River Canal won public support, but Kilbourn and Williams viewed the canal project as only the first step in the process of economic development that would in time lead to the establishment of a Milwaukee-Mississippi rail line. In 1836, Chicago promoters secured a charter for a railroad company to connect their city with the Mississippi, so the "race for greatness and supremacy" between the two lake ports had clearly begun.[6] Although Governor Doty killed Byron's plan for a Milwaukee and Rock River Canal in September of 1841, he told the legislature he, too, favored the idea of a Mississippi railroad. Three months later, Increase Lapham excitedly told his relatives, "We begin to talk railroads in Wisconsin!"[7]

All this talk notwithstanding, the territorial legislature voted down a bill to incorporate a Milwaukee to Mississippi line on February 10, 1842. Apparently many lawmakers were wary of Eastern capitalists who might

Alexander Mitchell, Scottish banker who founded the Milwaukee Road.

exercise monopoly control, a fear that later became a staple of populism in the Midwest. As one transportation historian observed, "No section of the country surpassed the West in enthusiasm for railroads."[8] It is not difficult to understand why. The new mode of transportation was considered to be the coming thing, and westerners wanted to be a part of that. The vast distances they faced in getting their crops to market made a fast, reliable form of transportation especially attractive. Byron Kilbourn meant to be in the center of the action. Accordingly, "No man in Wisconsin ... made so many railroad speeches, or has so often presided over State and District Conventions."[9]

The Panic of 1837 postponed any action on this front. Still, the dream remained alive in the minds of many. By 1844, Lapham declared that in his judgment, a railroad to the Mississippi was "entirely practicable." That same year, Byron Kilbourn decided to run for the territorial house, "to defend his continued attachment to the canal grant," and to persuade the legislature to transfer the canal grant he won to a Milwaukee-Mississippi railroad he intended to build.[10] In 1845, Asa Whitney proposed a transcontinental road be built clear to the Pacific, beginning in Wisconsin.[11] Railroading was everywhere in the air. Even *Sentinel* editor Rufus King embraced the idea, suggesting a "town tax" to fund a line from Milwaukee to Waukesha.[12]

Kilbourn's canal had its advocates and its

Rufus King, editor of the Milwaukee Sentinel

opponents. So, too, did his plan for a railroad. Nonetheless, a line to the Mississippi had great appeal in the coastal city as a way to foster growth, increase the value of local investments, and provide a commercial outlet for the products of the hinterland. Starting in 1836, the Wisconsin legislature chartered eight different railroad companies, none of which was ever built. The distinction of being the first line completed was reserved for Kilbourn's Milwaukee and Waukesha, incorporated February 11, 1847.

Milwaukee business leaders believed railroads were essential to their city's future. Many were prepared to invest heavily – conservative men of substance, such as the banker, Alexander Mitchell, John Tweedy, Kilbourn's former counsel, and Rufus King of the *Sentinel*. This time around, there were no Alanson Sweets or Harrison Reeds to object to Kilbourn's every move.

Everyone agreed that railroads were a good thing for Milwaukee and should be built as soon as possible. Early in 1847, Kilbourn circulated a document urging that *two lines* be built to the Mississippi, one starting in Chicago, the other in Milwaukee.[13] Under the guise of fairness he hoped to reserve Wisconsin's lucrative inland trade for his own city.

Businessman E. D. Holton recalled how matters stood at the time. Kilbourn's Milwaukee and Waukesha

Edward D. Holton, key supporter of the state's first railroad.

Railroad "was a great undertaking ... We were without money as a people, either in city or county. Every man had come to the county with limited means – and each had his house, his store, his shop, his barn to build, his land to clear and fence, and how could he spare anything from his own individual necessities?"

Yet the cause was irresistible. "It was demanded of our own people that they should lay aside all their feuds and personalities, and one and all join in the great work. To a very great extent this demand was complied with, and gentlemen were brought to work cordially and harmoniously together, who had stood aloof from each other for years." What's more, Holton continued, "the spirit of unity, harmony and concord exhibited by the people of the city was most cordially reciprocated by those of the country along the contemplated line of road."[14]

Mayor Joseph Goodrich of Milton who proposed using farm mortgages to fund railroad construction.

A sizable sum was subscribed, but actual cash payments were minimal. "I said we had no money," Holton said, "but we had things, and subscriptions were received with the understanding that they could be paid in such commodities as could be turned into the work of constructing the road. This method of building a railroad would be smiled at now, and was, by some among us, then. But it was after all a great source of our strength and of our success; at any rate for the time being." Construction began "in the fall of 1849, and for one entire year the grading was prosecuted and paid for by orders drawn upon the merchants, payable in goods – by carts from wagon makers, by harnesses from harness makers, by cattle, horses, beef, pork, oats, corn, potatoes and flour from the farmers, all received on account of stock subscriptions, and turned over to the contractors in payment of work done upon the road." Such bartering of goods served the country well enough in laying a roadbed, but who was to pay for the locomotives and the many iron rails needed? "Iron cost money," Holton noted, "and money we have not got. In this emergency, a mass meeting of stockholders was called at Waukesha, in the spring of 1850. About three hundred people assembled, mostly farmers. The question propounded was, how can $250,000 be obtained for the purchase of iron to reach from Milwaukee to Whitewater?"

Mayor Joseph Goodrich of Milton (southeast of Madison) came up with a novel solution. "See here; I can mortgage my farm for $3,000 and go to the east, where I came from, and get the money for it. Now, are there not one hundred men between Milwaukee and Rock River that can do the same?" There were, and hope ran high for an early completion to the project.[15] Edward Holton of Milwaukee and E. D. Clinton of Waukesha, canvassed the countryside for support, arguing that if Wisconsin's farmers failed to act, "foreign capitalists" would step forward. In this manner, $260,000 of railroad stock was sold.[16]

The Milwaukee and Waukesha Railroad Company was formally organized November 23, 1847. Dr. Lemuel Weeks was chosen president, and Alexander Mitchell, secretary. Among the nine board members named were John Tweedy and Byron Kilbourn. In February of 1848, Waukesha stock was put on sale in Milwaukee, at Byron Kilbourn's office. Promoters argued that Wisconsin traffic would flow to Chicago if their efforts to raise sufficient funds proved unsuccessful. Those most prominently identified with the line cut across party lines. Kilbourn was a "Free Soiler" (as he was soon to demonstrate at Buffalo); company lobbyist, Moses Strong, was a "regular" Democrat; both Rufus King and John Tweedy were prominent Whigs.

Article VIII, Section 10, of the new state constitution prohibited state investment in internal improvements, quite possibly a legacy of the territory's twelve-year struggle with the Milwaukee and Rock River Canal. Moreover, there was a widespread desire to avoid the indebtedness Wisconsin's neighbors incurred in this manner.[17] But the constitution did not prohibit a private company from seeking support from a municipality. On March 12, 1849, Byron Kilbourn was named, along with railroad supporters Mitchell, Tweedy, Kneeland, and Weeks, to draft a bill seeking Milwaukee Common Council support for the purchase of railroad stock. Five days later, the Wisconsin legislature authorized the city to purchase $100,000 in railroad securities, if it so wished. On May 19, Kilbourn was unanimously chosen to succeed Weeks as company president. The company itself was on the verge of bankruptcy, and it was rumored that the Chicago and Galena Railroad was about to build a spur line north to Fond du Lac, thereby draining off considerable inland trade from the city.

Kilbourn's major obstacle was financial, as it had been earlier with the canal. He needed cash, and he needed it at once. Direct state aid was unconstitutional. Use of the school fund, established when Wisconsin entered the Union, was denied by the legislature. An attempt by railroad counsel Moses Strong to secure a congressional land grant proved unsuccessful. An effort to transfer the property of the old canal grant to the Waukesha was also

Moses Strong, legislator and railroad lobbyist.

denied. And the new state was simply too poor to provide the capital necessary from private sources.

While he applauded the earnestness of Holton, Clinton, and Mayor Goodrich in securing farm mortgages in exchange for railroad stock, Kilbourn was wise to the ways of eastern capitalists. He suspected they would not provide the funds needed on the basis of unknown collateral. Thus, the Common Council represented his last hope. If he could persuade the Council members to exchange municipal bonds for farm mortgages, he might then have a security he could sell in eastern markets. Kilbourn served faithfully on the Council in 1846 and 1847, and as mayor in 1848 he presided over it. His credibility with this body was at an all-time high. He won his case. On July 19, 1849, the Council authorized the exchange to the extent of $100,000, the measure to be paid for with a 1 percent tax on real estate. Ultimately the City of Milwaukee's commitment to the Milwaukee and Waukesha, and later to the Milwaukee and Mississippi, rose to $234,000.[18]

On December 22, 1849, a meeting was called in Milwaukee to protest railroad funding. But railroad advocates outnumbered their opponents, so they simply took over the meeting. E. D. Holton was called to the chair, and Byron Kilbourn delivered the principal address. Kilbourn argued that trade in the city would decline without a railroad. He said that a city tax would not hurt the poor, as it would affect only real estate, not personal property. Railroad construction, he promised, would bring new jobs, and subsequent wages would allow the poor to purchase government land. The momentum in favor of a railroad was not to be denied.

There is a popular myth that history follows an orderly pattern. One is tempted to assume, for example, that railroads came readily to Wisconsin once the public recognized their worth. But such was not the case. The process of building Wisconsin's first line was fraught with obstacles, of which finance was the most formidable. Early in 1850, Kilbourn, acting on behalf of the Waukesha line, hired Assembly Speaker Moses Strong as a lobbyist. A former resident of Vermont, Strong had graduated from Dartmouth College and was trained in the law. Everyone recognized him as a gifted speaker. If anyone could persuade the people's representatives to subsidize the Waukesha line with money from the school fund, it was he. But despite a two-hour address designed for this purpose, Strong's best efforts were in vain; his funding proposal went down to defeat by a vote of 41 to 21.[19] Byron Kilbourn's involvement behind the scenes was alleged to be one of the reasons why.

At about this same time, the legislature allowed the Milwaukee and Waukesha to change its name to the Milwaukee and Mississippi.[20] After all, Kilbourn and his associates had this more extended route in mind all along. On January 31, 1850, the lawmakers also chartered a new corporation, called the Milwaukee and Rock River Plank Road Company. The proposed route of the new venture paralleled that of Kilbourn's old canal, which meant the plank road would become a reality should the much-discussed railroad fail to materialize. George Walker of Milwaukee's south side presided over the new firm.[21] There can be no doubt that Kilbourn was strongly committed to the completion of the Waukesha line. He and his wife, Henrietta, deeded $32,000 worth of property to the project, which made them the line's largest backers.

In April, railroad backers Holton and Tweedy deliberately misrepresented the state of the company's finances to local farmers.

The two claimed the company already had in hand sufficient funds to cover rail costs from Milwaukee to Waukesha and needed only additional revenue to extend the line to Whitewater. In fact, the company was at that moment some $3,000 in debt and was clearly dependent on new funds to complete the first part of the line. Were listeners to know the true state of company affairs, no one would purchase company stock. On May 8, Henry Dodge, having become one of Wisconsin's two U. S. Senators, proposed a congressional land grant so the line could be completed, but he was as unsuccessful as Strong had been earlier.[22]

Byron Kilbourn was then delegated to peddle Wisconsin farm mortgages in the east. He found, as he expected all along, that investors were unfamiliar with rural Wisconsin, and therefore unwilling to commit funds. But he also learned of a ready market for municipal bonds. If the Common Council could be persuaded to accept the farm mortgages in lieu of cash for its bonds, the bonds could then be converted into ready money. At the time, Milwaukee's residents tended to be "land rich and money poor." They figured that "if they could borrow what was requisite and build the line ... they could [quickly] pay off their notes and redeem their mortgages" – a gamble not unlike that taken by land speculators a generation earlier. Railroad backers "enthusiastically anticipated a tremendous economic expansion in Wisconsin," once state-of-the-art transportation facilities became available. "In an impious sort of modern alchemy, they hoped to convert their faith into good works."[23]

On June 10, Kilbourn returned from the east, and four days later he addressed a public meeting at the courthouse. He told his listeners that the roadbed to Waukesha was nearly complete, and that Tweedy and Clinton had raised about $300,000 in farm mortgages. He went on to say that he found no buyers for the mortgages in New York City, but that a market was there for *public securities*. Mayor Upham, in charge of the meeting, immediately appointed a committee of five pro-railroad men to draw up a resolution for Council approval. (One of these, of course, was Byron Kilbourn.) Although some present voiced opposition, the measure won the assent of the majority. A key actor in this drama was Dr. Francis Huebschmann, political leader of Milwaukee's growing German community.

The prevailing sentiment, on and off the Council, was strongly in favor of the railroad. Once the Council acted favorably on the committee resolution, Byron was again dispatched to New York City. This time his efforts met with success, and on July 16, he telegraphed his associates that he had disposed of the entire bond issue. "Bonfires blazed and cannons roared in our streets last night," the *Sentinel* reported, "... the day is not far distant when our Milwaukee Iron Horse, starting betimes from the shores of Lake Michigan, will slack his thirst at eve in the brimming Mississippi."[24]

Byron Kilbourn was the type of businessman who liked to control the action. Rather than delegate important tasks to others, he chose to do them himself. So when he secured the necessary funds to complete the line to Waukesha, he naturally chose to purchase the all-important locomotives personally. In late July he proceeded to Schenectady, New York, where he visited the local locomotive works. Walter Phelps, an employee of that firm, had contacted Jasper Vliet, a Kilbourn assistant, about a job in Milwaukee the preceding spring. Kilbourn now sought Phelps' assistance in buying sound engines for the Milwaukee-Waukesha run. The two men traveled to New York City and Syracuse to examine second-hand engines for sale before deciding to make their purchase at Schenectady, where they began their search. The locomotives, "Wisconsin" and "Iowa," were transported from Buffalo to Milwaukee on the brig *Abiah* and the schooner *Patrick Henry*. The twenty-ton locomotives were so heavy the Milwaukee River had to be dredged "close to the shore, so we could put long timbers to shore to vessel."

"I unloaded the two locomotives in a Lumber yard," Phelps later recalled. "The Wisconsin was landed September 12th, 1850 and the first run was made out about 1/2 mile past the Brick yard and back several times."[25]

On November 20, the engine made its major run to Waukesha and back. Regular passenger and freight service began five months later. Crowds cheered as "the brave little engine" pulled four passenger cars and one freight at the dizzying speed of ten miles an hour. Kilbourn himself laid out the track, "a twenty-one and a half mile route of almost unrivaled excellence [Byron reported], without a deep cut or high embankment, without a yard of rock excavation, and with only a few bridges of small dimensions."[26] A Vermonter, experienced in railroading, described the route rather differently. Kilbourn, he wrote home, "made a miserable location from Milwaukee to Waukesha, very crooked and about four miles out of the way."[27] Whichever view one accepts, the Milwaukee and Waukesha was an instant success, and the primary credit belongs to Byron Kilbourn, for it was he who built it.

The desire to micro-manage people and events led to Kilbourn's downfall soon after as president of the Milwaukee and Mississippi. According to one account, as workers began to lay track to Whitewater, Byron sought to take over the company. Secretly, he issued to a Waukesha henchman an "immense

Wisconsin's first locomotive.

amount" of stock, receiving only "one mill on the dollar in return," so that he could use the new shares to vote in his own board of directors. He was forestalled by the directors already on the board. On January 7, 1852, they removed him from the corporation's presidency, and thereafter he had no connection with the management of the Milwaukee and Mississippi.[28]

Byron's version of events was quite different, of course. At his own expense, he published a twenty-nine-page "defense" of his term as president. He said he sold $19,000 worth of railroad securities to contractor J. L. Bean of Waukesha. Bean, in turn, paid $1,900 down and promised to provide 20 percent of the remaining purchase price annually for five years thereafter. According to Byron, Bean was preparing to bid on a stretch of company line to the Wisconsin River, but the board acted first. They awarded the job to Selah Chamberlain of Cleveland, Ohio.[29] Byron makes no reference to a plan "to take over" the company, though it is clear a majority of the board members thought that was his intent. In his defense, Kilbourn describes his own efforts to preserve company credit by revoking a $100,000 loan by company treasurer Walter P. Flanders. And in the same document, he admits that the route he laid out between Milwaukee and Waukesha is crooked at times, but claims it was cheaper to build that way.

As he earlier attacked Alanson Sweet for opposing his canal plans, Kilbourn now singled out attorney John Tweedy for censure. Frustrated by the opposition of some of his fellow Milwaukeeans, Kilbourn vented his feelings openly:

> How long a house divided against itself can stand, is a problem likely to be tested in the history of Milwaukee. No important measure for the improvement of the business interest of our city has ever yet been begun or proposed, without arraying against it a strong, violent, and uncompromising opposition. The history of our Harbor, Canal, and Railroad, are great and imposing

LA CROSSE AND MILWAUKEE

RAILROAD.

DEPOT IN

SECOND WARD,

COR. OF CHESNUT AND THIRD STS.

La Crosse and Milwaukee Railroad broadside. Note that the Milwaukee depot for this line was formerly a part of Byron Kilbourn's business complex at Third and Chestnut. 1856-57 City Directory.

IN OPERATION TO BEAVER DAM,

[61 MILES.]

Passenger Trains leave the Depot in Milwaukee,
8.30 A. M. and 4 P. M.

Leave Beaver Dam 8 A. M. and 3 P. M.

Connect at Horicon, with Milwaukee and Horicon Railroad, completed to Waupun.

Connect at Junction with Chicago, St. Paul, and Fond du Lac Railroad, completed to Fond du Lac.

instances of this spirit, whereby the welfare of our city has been compromised, by the loss of millions of capital, which, by harmony and union of councils, might have been secured to our citizens, and would have been the means of placing Milwaukee in the first rank of Lake Cities.[30]

Kilbourn accused Flanders of fraud. The company board of directors disagreed. Kilbourn was removed from office; Flanders retained his post.

In December 1851, Wisconsin Senator Isaac Walker proposed that Congress grant land for the construction of a Milwaukee to

Mississippi railroad, the project envisioned by Kilbourn and Williams fifteen years earlier. The prospect of federal funds for such a line immediately caught Byron's eye. However, by January 1852, he was no longer affiliated with a railroad company (obviously a prerequisite if he were to compete for this prize). So he proceeded to create an entirely new company of his own. To this end, he hired Moses Strong to secure a charter for him. Byron, himself, kept a low profile, lest state legislators learn of his involvement and oppose the bill of incorporation. An adept politician, Strong did as he was told, and on April 2, 1852, "the La Crosse and Milwaukee Railroad" came into being.[31]

The La Crosse was controlled by a seven-member board of directors and was to operate at a capital fund of four million dollars accumulated through the sale of stock. Strong and Kilbourn were each rewarded for their start-up efforts with the presentation of a hundred paid shares of stock, and on August 25, Strong was elected president, and Kilbourn, chief engineer. The new company sent Strong to Washington to lobby for the passage of Senator Walker's bill. He did the best he could to entertain and woo the members of Congress, but to no avail. The bill failed to become law. The La Crosse would begin construction without federal assistance. In the fall and winter that followed, Strong traveled Wisconsin's frozen roads touting the advantages of his new firm and "Citizens ... subscribed over a quarter million dollars" toward the completion of a line from Milwaukee to the Mississippi.[32] The La Crosse made steady progress, reaching "Horicon in 1855, Portage in 1856, New Lisbon in 1857, and La Crosse [approximately 200 miles from Milwaukee] in 1858."[33] This goal was reached just a year after the Milwaukee and Mississippi completed its line to Prairie du Chien, further south.

Byron Kilbourn was an opportunist. He had vision, capital, and a sharp eye for ventures that promised a high return. He established a flour mill at Milwaukee at the very time when the city was on the verge of becoming the world's largest exporter of wheat. Kilbourn's investment was opportune for several reasons. The decade of the 1850s in Wisconsin was a decade of extensive railroad building. Hence, access to new markets was constantly growing. The decade was also a period of extensive immigration into the rural areas of the state, thus increasing the domestic market as well. And the invention of new farm equipment made wheat the state's primary agricultural crop. Wheat prices varied from year to year, ranging from a low of $0.60 per bushel to a high of $1.30. Flour also fluctuated, running from a low of $3.10 a bushel to a high of $6.70. By 1860, Milwaukee mills were exporting directly to markets in New York and New England. Volume soared from four million bushels in 1850 to well over fifteen million ten years later. By 1862, Milwaukee "had become the largest primary wheat market in the world."[34] The number of flouring mills in the city grew from three in 1850 to nineteen in 1860. By this latter date, flour was at a premium and its value to the Wisconsin economy was *twelve times as much* as any other Wisconsin commodity, except sawed lumber. In 1858, Milwaukee erected its first grain warehouse and elevator – at Byron Kilbourn's depot of the La Crosse Railroad. Although we do not know precisely how much money Kilbourn gained from his milling speculation, it seems likely the venture was highly profitable.

Two other investments that resulted from Byron's ties with the La Crosse Railroad merit our attention. The first of these involved the iron mines of Dodge County, an area lying about 45 miles northwest of the city of Milwaukee. In the summer of 1846, Chester and Eli May, father and son, brought a sample of their red soil to Milwaukee for analysis. Mayor Juneau burned "the sample in a crucible and with a magnet could take out 90% of it." He pronounced the substance "iron ore of the finest quality."[35] That same year, Increase Lapham published a new edition of his geography of the territory. Lapham reported that fragments of limonite (brown hermatite iron ore) had been found in Dodge County on the "ridges near the Rock River, but nothing is known of the quantity of the ore." Three years later in 1849, Charles Whittlesey, a Cleveland, Ohio, geologist, surveyed the Iron Ridge

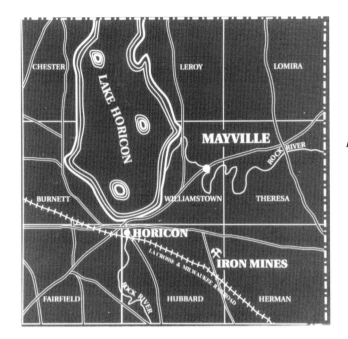

Map of iron deposits in Dodge County.

country. (This was the same man, incidentally, who interviewed James Kilbourn in 1845 for a biography he was preparing on John Fitch). Whittlesey confirmed that iron ore deposits existed, but he did not have the time necessary to determine its exact size. He did report, however, that iron is "already exposed in sufficient quantities to make it a certain supply for a long time, and theoretically it should occupy extensive tracts, where it is not visible, to the south and east." Shortly thereafter, the Wisconsin Iron Company began producing twelve tons of molten ore a day.

Byron Kilbourn purchased the site of the Wisconsin Iron Company in 1853, and in the next six years, he bought over 3,000 acres of potentially rich mineral land in the area. In March of 1854, he co-founded the Swedes Iron Company and the Washington Iron Company. Two years later, he established the Iron Ridge and Mayville Railroad Company, a spur line connecting his mine holdings with the nearby tracks of his La Crosse and Milwaukee Railroad. Anticipating extensive operations, the Swedes Iron

Chester May, who discovered iron ore in Dodge County in 1845.

Company quadrupled its capital stock from $600,000 to $2.4 million. But the best-laid plans sometimes go astray. The Panic of 1857 intervened, followed four years later by the outbreak of the Civil War. Mining did not actually start at Kilbourn's site until 1864, and then, only after Byron supplied a start-up loan of $50,000.

The secretary of the Swedes Iron Company was Havens Cowles, Rensselaer Cowles' oldest son and Byron's nephew by his first wife. Cowles played a key role in company activities, preparing a persuasive brochure designed to lure prospective investors. The first shipment of iron ore to Milwaukee by the company occurred August 20, 1864, when 620 tons were forwarded. By late fall, the company sent 2,592 tons south, 2,370 of which went by water to Cleveland, Ohio, for processing. When mining operations began, the company's stockholders numbered six: three from Connecticut, one from New Jersey, one from New York – and Wisconsin's Byron Kilbourn.

Apparently, the company practiced open-pit mining. Charles J. Woolson, with whom Kilbourn entered into a mining contract, reported that "the iron ore on the property was ... so plentiful that it could be loaded into wagons 'as easily as common earth.'"

On June 18, 1868, the smelting works and iron furnace of the company were destroyed by fire, resulting in a loss of $70,000. But the company quickly rebuilt, and a year later established its own rolling mill at Milwaukee. On June 29, 1869, the Swedes Iron Company was sold to an Illinois-Michigan combine for $500,000, the largest real estate transaction ever recorded in Dodge County. If we assume that the original six partners were still active, Byron Kilbourn's share of this venture probably amounted to about $83,000.

We do not know exactly how much money Kilbourn made from this speculation, though it seems likely it was substantial, perhaps as much as $100,000. We do know that in 1855 when one ton of pig iron elsewhere cost $6 to $7, the Dodge County mines could produce the same amount for $0.25 per ton.

Kilbourn's Iron Ridge furnace was the only one west of Indiana designed to produce pig iron. Moreover, the company had ready access by means of Kilbourn's La Crosse Railroad to Milwaukee, plus an ore elevator for storage and for the loading of lake vessels – all in all, an admirable delivery system. Consumer demand for iron products was great, and increasing; how could one lose?

According to the *Milwaukee City Directory* for 1865, the Swedes Iron Company "own an extensive bed of ore ... and contemplate bringing the product of the same to Milwaukee, both for shipment and manufacture of pig and railroad iron. The only labor in getting the ore is that of loading it upon the cars, just as

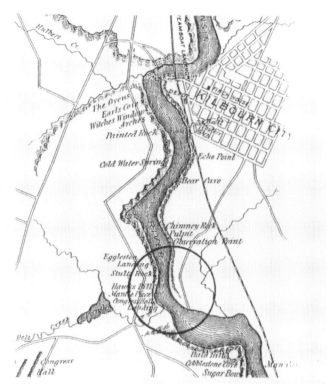

Map of Kilbourn City showing the Newport region to the south (circled).

sand would be shoveled out of a sand pit. It is in fine particles like sand, and can be elevated by machinery and loaded into vessels in the same manner as grain, an elevator having been erected for the purpose at the terminus of the La Crosse and Milwaukee Railroad [beside Byron's home in Milwaukee] ... This ore is of a very superior quality, yielding 42 per cent of pure iron, almost as hard as steel, and when mixed in the proportion of three to one with the fibrous iron of Lake Superior, it makes an excellent quality of railroad iron."

Kilbourn's timing deserves comment. How is it possible that a businessman would begin a new venture in 1864 in the midst of war? Was he motivated by a sense of patriotism, or government need? Neither assumption is correct. Contrary to normal expectation, the Wisconsin economy flourished in wartime, even though its Mississippi route to the Gulf was closed to commercial traffic. What happened is that the state's railroads, completed in the fifties, replaced shipping as the key means of transportation to the east and south. By August of 1864, the outcome of the war was no longer in doubt. The high tide of the Confederacy had passed, and the North would ultimately triumph because of superior resources and manpower. It was only a matter of time. Businessmen like Byron Kilbourn turned their thoughts to the future, to the probable needs of a country moving ever westward. Kilbourn was a believer in railroads early on, and thought one day soon there would be one or more transcontinental lines.[36] In fact, the first railroad to span the continental United States was completed five years later. As everyone knew, railroads required high quality iron, the very product Kilbourn could supply in abundance.[37] Hundreds of miles of track would be needed. Byron meant to be a major supplier of a product in great demand. Rail access from the mines in Dodge County to Milwaukee was assured by 1855. Although Byron's plans for iron mining were delayed, first by depression and then by war, his speculation was ultimately successful. He spent a substantial sum to acquire control of an important mineral resource and profited accordingly.

Kilbourn City Railroad Depot.

Byron Kilbourn as he appeared in the 1850s.

A second example of railroad-connected investment involved the settlement of what is today called Wisconsin Dells, a town in the central part of the state on the Wisconsin River. In 1849, Joseph Bailey, a citizen of Galena, Illinois, decided to move his family to the east bank of the Wisconsin River at the lower dells (or rapids), a point fifty-two miles northwest of the city of Madison. Others joined him, and soon there was the nucleus of a promising community. Bailey, and a young attorney by the name of Jonathan Bowman, secured title to 400 acres of land at the river's edge. In the tradition of frontier speculators elsewhere, they thought big and dreamed of a city of 10,000. They called their settlement "Newport" in honor of the fact that at high water, steamships from the Mississippi could actually navigate all the way to their door.[38]

In 1850, the Wisconsin legislature approved a charter for a bridge to span the river at Newport and authorized the construction of a dam as well. But residents based their greatest hope for prosperity on the building of an east-west railroad; namely, Byron Kilbourn's La Crosse and Milwaukee. Citizens were convinced that if the new line ran through Newport, the future of their town would be assured. To this end, Bailey and Bowman entered into an agreement with Kilbourn, the railroad's president. In exchange for the railroad coming through their town, the two deeded over to him 200 acres of their original spread. The incorporators of the dam also signed their charter over to Kilbourn with the understanding that he or a company he chose would undertake its construction. Garrett Vliet was Kilbourn's agent in the negotiations, the same Vliet who laid out Kilbourntown in Milwaukee in 1835. As part of the agreement, Vliet promised to oversee a plat survey of the hitherto uncharterted acreage. He and Kilbourn also signed two bonds of $100,000 each, "providing that in case the road should not cross the river at this point, that amount should be forfeited ... to cover damages sustained by the parties executing the deed and transfer."[39]

Work began. Vliet and five others established a "Wisconsin River Hydraulic Company," and it was this firm that Kilbourn chose to build the dam. In anticipation of imminent prosperity, Newport real estate prices soared, in some cases selling for ten times their original purchase price. Some property owners "doubled their money in 24 hours," and those who owned property that would be flooded when the dam was built boasted of the high prices they intended to charge the company for their holdings.

Joseph Bailey, co-founder of Newport.

Kilbourn and Vliet then asked Bailey and Bowman for the return of their security bonds; "grading had been completed on the railroad right of way west of the river and substantial work had been done on the dam; therefore the request of the makers of the bonds was granted." But it so happened that the law authorizing placement of the dam gave "broad discretion" to the builder as to precise location; the dam could be erected in any one of three

Jonathan Bowman, co-founder of Newport and later one of
Byron Kilbourn's land agents in Kilbourn City.

sections in two different counties! Acting on this flexible provision, the Hydraulic Company bypassed Newport entirely in favor of an alternate site. In 1855, Vliet's Hydraulic Company quietly purchased a town site two miles north of Newport.

Shortly thereafter, an eastern newspaperman by the name of Alanson Holly began the area's first newspaper, the *Wisconsin Mirror*. But instead of establishing his printing office in the flourishing town of Newport, Holly settled in the uninhabited woods two miles north of town ... on land deeded him by the Hydraulic Company. Holly was made a director of the company, and in February 1856 the company agreed to defray the expenses of his newspaper. February was also the month in which Holly reported that the new dam would be built north of town rather than in Newport itself. The reason given for the site change was that the upper location was better suited topographically. On June 10, 1856, Holly proposed that the new community be called Kilbourn City in honor of the Milwaukeean who played so key a role in its establishment. That name prevailed until 1931 when it was changed to Wisconsin Dells.

Did Kilbourn, Vliet, Holly and their cohorts engage in a conspiracy to commit fraud? The answer to this important question varies depending on whose interpretation you accept. E. C. Dixon analyzed the matter this way in 1942: "Whether there was at that time an actual purpose to commit fraud or whether later events only made it appear that such might have been the case, only the opening of the books on Judgment Day will ever reveal." He claimed the evidence was circumstantial, that the reason given for a change in the location of the dam made sense, that inflated land prices might well have caused Kilbourn and others to favor an alternative location, and that secrecy in the purchase of the Kilbourn City site may have been only a matter of business precaution. The head of the local historical society presents a different version: "I believe Alanson Holly was a cohort of Byron Kilbourn, in a conspiracy which led to the demise of the city of Newport, and the creation of Wisconsin Dells."[40] A satirical broadside was published at Kilbourn City, November 2, 1858. Framed as a playbill, the sheet advertises eleven acts, involving parodies of those connected with the railroad bridge, dam, and new town. "The great immortal Byron" is featured as star and master of ceremonies.[41] Assigning motives to behavior after the fact is always risky. We do know, however, that Kilbourn perceived the Wisconsin River area to be a promising locale for future development. In 1865, a decade after the founding of Kilbourn City, he held title to 154 acres of land in Sauk County, 340 in Columbia County, and 304 in Adams County.[42]

The Kilbourn City episode is further evidence of Kilbourn's aggressive opportunism. Those who prospered with him thought he could do no wrong; those whose dreams were destroyed were bitter in their denunciation of the man. That

Kilbourn personally controlled the location of the railroad and the dam seems certain. Joseph Bailey, the defeated Newport speculator, moved north to Kilbourn City and "built a fine home there," but he clearly felt Kilbourn and Holly had deceived him.[43]

The Dells bridge was completed in 1857, destroyed by fire in 1866, and rebuilt soon after. Byron often rode back and forth from Milwaukee to Kilbourn City on business in the 1860s. At the time of his death at age sixty-nine in 1870, he held title to 218 lots within the community. Byron's obituary, published by the *Kilbourn City Mirror*, runs as follows: "To him, in a large degree, the town owes its being. Through his influence, the railroad and dam were secured to this place, which attracted attention and really started the town."

Internal improvements came slowly to the Wisconsin Territory. In the aftermath of the Panic of 1837, little was accomplished, and with the demise of Kilbourn's canal, all thought of major transportation improvements was put on hold. But by 1850, the economy had revived. Milwaukee was more than two-thirds the size of Chicago,"and the projected transit route across the lake from Milwaukee to Grand Haven [Michigan] gave promise of bypassing Chicago in trade flowing to and from the Northwest."[44] Unfortunately, winter ice prevented dependable year-round service. Moreover, in the decade of the 1850s, Chicago's railroads, led by the Illinois Central with its link to Mobile on the Gulf, flourished beyond all expectation. By the outbreak of the Civil War, Chicago could boast eleven lines, and the city was clearly dominant over its Wisconsin rival. The prize that Milwaukee and Chicago vied for was nothing less than the commercial leadership of the upper Midwest. Byron Kilbourn intended to use every means possible to win this prize for himself and his city. As Milwaukee prospered, so did his extensive real estate investments.

Chicago capitalists looked upon the produce of Wisconsin, Iowa, and Minnesota, with envy. In 1852, William Ogden's fledgling Chicago and North Western gained control of a line into Wisconsin as far north as Fond du Lac, and Ogden hungered for a larger share of the pie. Meanwhile, the Wisconsin legislature chartered 45 new railroad companies in 1853 alone. The success of Kilbourn's Milwaukee and Waukesha, two years earlier, made railroads appear to be the achievable dream of the decade. In February of 1854, Congress debated a bill that would provide two land grants to Wisconsin for railroad construction.[45] A northeast line was projected to extend from the Illinois state line north through Janesville and Fond du Lac to Lake Superior. A northwest line was to run from Janesville through Madison to the St. Croix River. Congressman Daniel Wells of Milwaukee opposed the bill outright, since it did nothing for his city. Congressman Eastman of Rock County was also opposed, for he felt the existing Milwaukee and Mississippi Railroad failed to meet local needs. Some members of the House of Representatives argued that all land grants were unconstitutional. Others thought they were a waste of public land, and still others maintained that such bills were unfair to the older states of the Union. Given such diverse opposition, the bill went down to defeat.

Not until June 3, 1856, twenty-seven months later, did the deed get done. The bill President Pierce signed into law was significantly different from its predecessor. The two projected routes were considerably altered. The northeastern route, formerly the longer and more lucrative of the two, was shortened to run from Fond du Lac north to the Michigan state line. The northwestern route, on the other hand, was lengthened to run from Madison north by way of Portage to the St. Croix, and then on to the western end of Lake Superior. Spur lines were to be extended to Columbus and Bayfield. The company that won the grant was "to have every alternate section of land ... for six sections in width on each side of the line." Government parcels, as in the earlier Milwaukee and Rock River Canal grant, "were to be held for sale at double the minimum price [i.e. $2.50 per acre]. The intent of this proviso was to reduce the monetary loss to the national government."[46]

Railroad attorney Moses Strong estimated at the time that the northwest grant was worth some $17 million, an *astronomincal sum* in antebellum days. At stake in the northwest grant alone were more than a million acres of government land, easily the largest financial plum in the young state's history.

Chicagoan William Ogden led the lobbying efforts in Washington on behalf of the 1856 Wisconsin bill. Shortly after the bill became law, he traveled to Madison to collect

William Ogden, Chicago businessman who founded the Chicago and Northwestern Railroad.

his reward; he asked the Wisconsin legislature to award BOTH GRANTS to his Chicago and North Western line. Were Ogden to get his wish, Chicago would dominate interior traffic throughout the state, and Milwaukee, Wisconsin's largest city, would be completely bypassed. The Wisconsin legislature, given this prospect, denied Ogden's request. They held that *Wisconsin companies should be the ones to develop Wisconsin railroads*. To meet the requirements of the northeast grant, a new company was created, called the Wisconsin and Superior. Byron Kilbourn's La Crosse and Milwaukee was one of several contenders for the other prize.

In late May of 1856, a week after the congressional bill had been approved, a group of men met at the Walker House in Milwaukee to form an association "the legal, honorable and commendable object" of which is to obtain the northwest grant for the La Crosse and Milwaukee. Among the group were Byron Kilbourn, president of the La Crosse and Milwaukee Railroad,

Moses Strong, attorney for the La Crosse Company, former governor William Barstow, his lieutenant governor Arthur MacArthur, and James Knowlton. Early in August, the association, by this time including former governor James Doty, "met again to put their agreement in writing, and at this meeting Strong was chosen chairman of a committee to draft a bill to be presented to the Legislature..."[47] "The list of 'associates' was virtually a who's who of Wisconsin's most prominent citizens. It included the three ex-governors of the state – Nelson Dewey, Leonard J. Farwell and William A. Barstow – as well as leading lawyers, businessmen, [newspaper] editors and legislators." James Doty "was appointed a member of a steering committee of six to keep things moving; he was also delegated to guide the voting of five specified legislators from the northeast."[48] Prior politics were put aside as Wisconsin's leaders of public opinion united to guarantee that the northwest grant would go to Byron Kilbourn's company, and that Wisconsin's longest rail line would be developed by a bona fide Wisconsin company.

Keep in mind that railroad fever had swept the state. Milwaukeeans, in particular, were ready to tolerate "whatever cost in money or political ethics" to win the northwest land grant. As one historian later noted, "seldom has a more attractive prize been dangled before the eyes of promoters than this grant constituted."[49] Initially, there were four contenders; Byron Kilbourn narrowed the odds by buying out two of them: the Milwaukee and Watertown, and the St. Croix and Lake Superior. He was unable to reach an accommodation with his former company, the Milwaukee and Mississippi. Kilbourn's strategy in opposing Ogden's Chicago and North Western bid was to couch his appeal in terms of state loyalty. Wisconsin railroads should be built by Wisconsin companies, his argument ran. At the time, Ogden's company was alleged to have purchased the votes of fifteen state legislators, thereby assuring *he* would win the grant. No proof of this allegation has ever been found, but the circumstantial evidence is certainly suggestive. The Chicago and North Western was so confident of victory, it did not enter the race seriously until late in September, at a point when it seemed likely the special session of the legislature would favor Kilbourn's La Crosse Company. A student of the land grant case offers the following trenchant observation: "That the Chicago, St. Paul and Fond du Lac Company [the parent of the Chicago and North Western] would not have been above bribing the Legislature was proved by the investigation of *the northeastern grant*, which revealed the conspiracy whereby the directors of the Wisconsin and Superior Railroad Company which had been incorporated by the Legislature to receive the northeastern grant, resigned their positions in favor of men representing the Chicago company."[50] This act of legerdemain cost Ogden's firm $102,500.

The practice of accepting favors in exchange for legislative support was common in Kilbourn's day, and still occurs from time to time in our own. But never in the history of Wisconsin was it implemented on so great a scale. Consider the facts. In September and October of 1856, Kilbourn, Moses Strong, and their associates courted Madison lawmakers and other influential opinion leaders, promising "liberal compensation" should the La Crosse Company be awarded the land grant. The gratuity was to be in the form of La Crosse Company bonds, deliverable upon the recording of a favorable vote. The recipients of this largesse and the face value of the securities they were to receive is as follows:

Governor Coles Bashford $50,000
13 State Senators $175,000
(only one of whom refused)
59 Members of the Assembly $355,000
(the amount ranged from $5,000 to $20,000 apiece)
26 opinion leaders $281,000
(including the lieutenant governor, the governor's private secretary, chief clerk and assistant clerk of the Assembly, plus such business leaders as Alexander Mitchell and Rufus King)

Twelve of twenty-three members of the Senate received gifts, along with fifty-nine of seventy Assemblymen. The vote in favor of awarding the land grant to the La Crosse Company was 17 to 6 in the Senate, and 63 to 7 in the Assembly. In an effort to secure the prize, $861,000 of company securities were distributed.[51] *Fewer than 5 percent of those offered certificates refused them.* The most famous legislator who did was State Senator Amasa Cobb, who was approached by the assistant clerk of the Assembly on the company's behalf. Asked what would induce him to support the La Crosse land grant bill, Cobb replied that if Byron Kilbourn "would multiply the capital stock of the company [ten million dollars] by the number of leaves in the Capitol Park, and give me that amount in money," and then have himself, Moses Strong, and Alexander Mitchell "blacked, and give me a clear title to them as servants for life, I would take the matter under consideration." Upon the reporting of this exchange, the Senator was ever after known throughout the state as "Honest" Amasa Cobb.[52]

The Chicago and North Western officials soon became "fearful of losing the grant." James H. Knowlton, one of the original participants at the meetings in Milwaukee, "shifted his allegiance to the Chicago company." Knowlton advised his fellow Assemblymen at Madison that "men were bragging in the streets that they had bought up a majority of the legislature."[53] But the protests of the Chicago faction fell on deaf ears. On October 9 the legislature voted to award the northwest land grant to Byron Kilbourn's La Crosse and Milwaukee Railroad.

Ogden's firm was not to be denied its day in court, however. For if the La Crosse grant were revoked, Ogden might yet win the prize. Josiah Noonan, an anti-Kilbourn leader who happened to be Milwaukee's postmaster, and Horace Tenney, a leading newspaper editor in Madison, joined forces with Ogden's lobbyists to demand a legislative investigation. "Noonan flooded the state with petitions and Tenney promised to engineer the investigation in the Legislature." Kilbourn "knew an investigation would depress the market" for his railroad bonds, so he and Moses Strong "bought" Tenney off.[54] The push for a hearing was halted ... temporarily. But the allegations concerning a bribery scandal drew widespread attention. *Harper's Magazine*, a New York publication with a large readership nationwide, ran a cartoon depicting a "conscientious railroad president [obviously Kilbourn], purchasing public officials in the "political market."[55] To be sure, corruption existed elsewhere in the country, but not on such a lavish scale. Something had to be done to salvage the state's reputation.

On January 15, 1858, incoming Governor Alexander Randall, addressed the legislature on the topic. "Grave charges have been made in the past year," he declared, alleging "corrupt conduct in the Legislature ... good citizens have become alarmed at such official misconduct, and the reputations of the members of that Legislature, and of the State have naturally suffered in consequence." Randall declared that "the man who would dare to approach a sworn public officer with a bribe to turn him from his honest conviction of duty, should be hunted down by the law and severely punished."[56] And so, "on February 1, 1858, after nearly two years of agitation, the Legislature passed a bill creating a joint committee to investigate the charges." Joint Resolution 6-A reads in part as follows: "That a joint committee, composed of three members of the Senate, and five of the Assembly, be raised, whose duty should be, fully and impartially, to investigate into the frauds, bribery, and corrupt acts, reported or alleged to have been perpetuated or committed, by members of the legislature, or others, in the disposal, or in the procuring the disposal by the legislature of this State, in the year eighteen hundred and fifty-six, of the lands granted to this State, to aid in the construction of railroads, by act of Congress . . . ."

In retrospect, it is clear that while both Democrats and Republicans accepted gratuities from either the Chicago or Milwaukee railroad companies, neither wished to oppose the investigation; both hoped they might use the inquiry to smear their opponents. The joint committee was given the power to subpoena witnesses, but the enabling bill also stated that "*no person testifying before the committee would be held to answer criminal charges*, and testimony would not be used against a witness, except upon prosecution for perjury"[57] [emphasis added].

With so many legislators personally involved, an impartial hearing was unlikely at best, and when James Knowlton (by then an attorney for the Chicago and North Western), was made committee chair, and Horace Tenney, secretary, the outcome of the inquiry was no longer in doubt. The investigation was to be a witch hunt, not a search for truth. Lawmakers seemed less concerned that bribery took place than with discovering the means devised to conceal the activity.[58]

At first, Byron Kilbourn and Assemblyman Thomas Falvey refused to testify before the committee, but the State Supreme Court "denied them writs of *habeas corpus*" so they had no choice in the matter. The hearings were held before an overflow audience at the state capitol in February, March, and April of 1858. While the circumstances surrounding the deposition of both land grants were explored, "Knowlton and Tenney channeled the investigation safely away from themselves and their associates, and pointed the finger of shame at the La Crosse and Milwaukee. The investigation ended May 13 with the reading before the legislature of the long awaited report. It contained no startling disclosures." As the *Madison Argus* put it, the committee "proved what everybody knew long ago, but have done nothing about. They wasted public funds – about $30,000 – to prove people rascals, proved it, and left the rascals just where they found them."[59]

Byron Kilbourn's version of events was, of course, quite different. At his own expense, he published a sixty-page "review" of the investigating committee report.[60] His case was divided into six parts: the committee report itself; bribery, fraud, and corruption; charges against the La Crosse Company; charges against himself; the role played by James Knowlton; and general remarks. Starting with the report itself, Kilbourn charged that minimal attention was given William Ogden's takeover of the northeast grant, while his own company was "held up to the world as having been guilty of the basest offenses, and therefore unworthy of public confidence." Kilbourn maintained that the committee's function was to report facts and collect testimony, not draw conclusions. This, he argued, was the job of the legislature itself. In essence, he said, "the Committee erected themselves into a Court and Jury." Further, he noted the legislature took no action whatever on committee recommendations. Turning to the charge of bribery, Kilbourn argued from definition that bribery had not taken place at all. The compensation given the supporters of the land grant bill, he said, was not provided to change the votes of members, because they fully intended to back the bill anyway. As a case in point, Senator Chappell had told his colleagues he would vote for the La Crosse bill without a gratuity, "because I then believed it right so to do, and I was so instructed by my constituents." Had William Ogden's Chicago company received both grants, all the benefits of Wisconsin commerce would flow south to the Illinois city. It was the *duty*, Kilbourn said, of Wisconsin's legislators to award both grants to Wisconsin firms. "It does not impair the integrity of their conduct," Kilbourn claimed, "that they subsequently received a gratuity or a consideration from the La Crosse Company, which they may have done very honestly. Having first discharged their duty faithfully to the State, they may have considered the benefits accruing to the Company such that the latter could well afford a small renumeration for favors received." Since members did not vote contrary to their convictions, Kilbourn argued, "there was neither bribery or fraud committed." Kilbourn estimated the La Crosse grant was worth $20 million. A "reasonable" commission of 2.5 percent would amount to $500,000, so he considered the amount of bonds actually tendered "moderate." Byron next reviewed his company's efforts to secure the grant. He confirmed the two association meetings in Milwaukee, and the plan of those present to use "their personal influence" with legislators to secure passage of the bill. He admitted that he was the author of the original bill, and said that Assemblyman Knowlton drafted a new version so that company directors could later be replaced by Ogden appointees, the strategy used earlier to secure the northeast grant. Kilbourn charged that Ogden's company intended to secure the northwest grant for a consideration of $1.5 million ($100,000 for each of fifteen carefully selected legislators), though he was unable to supply any proof of this. He admitted that the La Crosse Company bought out the rival Watertown Railroad as a means of limiting competition.

The heart of Kilbourn's defense lay in his argument that without the La Crosse entry into the land grant sweepstakes, both grants would have ended up in Chicago hands. "No bribe was either offered or received," he wrote. "In all our intercourse with members, we argued the question upon the merits alone. They did their duty as has already been shown, faithfully and conscientiously to the State, and I know of no law, human or divine, which should prevent the directors from giving, or the members of the legislature from receiving, the inconsiderable gratuities which were made." The gratuities Byron considered "inconsiderable," others saw as substantial. Kilbourn noted that Ogden's company spent $64,000 in Washington lobbying for the Wisconsin grants, and that Ogden asked the La Crosse Company, of which Kilbourn was president, to pay that bill when it won the northwest grant. (There is no evidence that they did so.)

Kilbourn's analysis of the attacks upon himself merit particular attention. Therefore they are cited here at length:

> It has been my fortune, or misfortune, on many occasions, to cross the path of ambitious and aspiring persons, and of course [I] have been more or less assailed by them. Nearly all my sins of this nature however have been in connection with the internal improvements of the country and only so far mixed up with political matters as became necessary to carrying out these projects. But this was sufficient to bring me in contact and some-times in conflict with politicians, though having no political aspirations of my own to gratify.

Politicians as a general rule, are a sensitive and jealous race of people, and being prone to judge others by themselves, imagine that all men are so constituted that they would sacrifice the substantial good of the world, to a bauble. I have unfortunately sometimes run athwart the plans of some of these gentlemen, and have, therefore, as a matter of course, been made the object of their attacks. In such cases where only myself personally was concerned, I have generally left it to *time*, to furnish the refutation of unjust assaults, and to vindicate my acts. But when these attacks have involved the welfare of important measures in which I was concerned, or the reputation of my friends, I have some times taken the trouble to make a formal refutation. I have often been blamed by my friends, for not taking more pains to refute unfounded amputations against myself when it was perfectly easy to do so; but my answer had been that if my life and acts will not vindicate me, there [can] be no vindication. My faith is, that time will set all things right, and when circumstances shall no longer furnish a motive for detraction, even my enemies will do me justice.[61]

Four groups opposed the La Crosse grant, Kilbourn said: "a Milwaukee clique" long opposed to any improvement he favored, Democrats who feared that his success in securing the grant would result in his and his supporters' controlling party affairs for years to come, rival railroad companies, both in and outside the state, and New York stockholders of the La Crosse Company, who hoped the company would foreclose so they could secure its control at a fraction of its true value. He noted that the City of Milwaukee alone invested $300,000 in his firm, the bulk of which would be lost if foreclosure were to take place.

On October 29, 1857, Byron resigned the company presidency, saying that he was happy to retire "from a position, which had been to me only a source of anxiety and laborious effort, and of personal sacrifice." He reported that eastern investors demanded that they be given majority membership on the board of directors, as they controlled a majority of company stock. (In much the same fashion, Morgan Martin of Green Bay was eased out of the leadership of the Fox-Wisconsin Improvement Company he founded.)

Whatever the truth of Byron's assertions, his defense won him little support, and primary responsibility for the land grant scandal "came to rest" upon his shoulders. Moses Strong spent six days and nights in the Dane County Jail for refusing to cooperate with the investigating committee. But Kilbourn received no fines and served no time. Instead, his punishment was the permanent loss of his good name. After 1858, he ceased to play a major role in the affairs of the company he founded and the state he attempted to serve.[62]

Kilbourn denied he personally profited from company largesse. He said that he had returned $25,000 worth of railroad stock granted him for "extra services" in securing the land grant, and that he had applied a second award of $50,000 toward the payment of the debt the company owed him for its railroad depot at Chestnut and Third. While it may be true that Byron did not enrich himself at the expense of the company treasury, he clearly profited from his iron ore speculation in Dodge County and his real estate holdings at Kilbourn City. Perhaps it is only human nature for us to want to blame someone when our hopes are destroyed. Although "20 to 30" prominent Milwaukeeans were as active as he in lobbying for the La Crosse grant, Kilbourn, alone, was singled out for blame. With the exception of Governor Bashford, who converted his railroad bonds into cash before fleeing to Arizona, most of the "rascals" profited not at all from their gratuities, for the La Crosse went into receivership the same year the legislature released its findings.

The State of Wisconsin authorized publication of 5,000 copies of the investigating committee report, a document which came to be known as the infamous "Black Book." Almost overnight, the copies disappeared, taken up, some said, by those whose names appeared there as "bribery" recipients. The economic Panic of 1857 destroyed both La Crosse and Mississippi and the Milwaukee and Mississippi.

Byron Kilbourn had figured prominently in Wisconsin affairs for more than twenty years during which time he accumulated a host of enemies: farmers who mortgaged their land so his canal and railroads could be built, rival speculators with competing interests of their own, eastern investors who hoped to make a fortune overnight, only to face the hard reality of economic depression and lost income, and Chicago speculators anxious to capture Wisconsin's trade for themselves. Railroad companies at the time were often poorly managed, and some officials were corrupt. Promoters promised more than they could deliver. For all who were disgruntled, Byron Kilbourn became the symbol of frustration, failure, greed and immorality. It was as if public opinion demanded a scapegoat, and Kilbourn fit the bill.

The plan to sell millions of acres of government land to fund construction of a rail line to Lake Superior failed, and it was another decade before Alexander Mitchell picked up the pieces and established the highly successful Milwaukee Road. Ironically, Mitchell was one of those who accepted Kilbourn's "liberal compensation."

Endnotes

[1] Buck, *Pioneer History* I, 131; Barnum, "Public Aid," p. 1. Fitch's model is now on display at the Ohio Historical Center in Columbus.

[2] Berquist and Bowers, *The New Eden*, pp. 207-208.

[3] H. Burnham to Micajah Williams, March 20, 1835, OHC, Williams Papers.

[4] MCHS, Lapham Papers.

[5] William F. Raney, "The Building of Wisconsin's Railroads," *Wisconsin Magazine of History*, XIX, No. 4 (June 1936), 387.

[6] Barnum, "Public Aid," p. 7.

[7] December 7, 1841, MCHS, Lapham Papers.

[8] *Transportation Revolution*, p. 93.

[9] *History of Milwaukee, Wisconsin*, II, 1176.

[10] *Wisconsin*, p. 313; Barnum, "Public Aid," p. 39.

[11] Smith, *Doty*, p. 326; Barnum, "Public Aid," pp. 46-47.

[12] *Ibid.*, p. 61; Holton, "Commercial History," pp. 275-276.

[13] Barnum, "Public Aid," p. 54.

[14] "Commercial History," p. 276.

[15] *Ibid.*, p. 277.

[16] William F. Raney, *Wisconsin: A Story of Progress* (New York: Prentice Hall, 1940). p. 181.

[17] Larson, *Financial History*, p. 50.

[18] *Ibid.*, pp. 80-81.

[19] The actual date was February 1, 1850. Barnum, "Public Aid," p. 50.

[20] *Ibid.*, p. 85.

[21] *Ibid.*, p. 86.

[22] *Ibid.,* p. 90.

[23] *Ibid.*, p. 90.

[24] *Ibid.*, pp. 107-108.

[25] For a detailed account of Kilbourn's purchase of the locomotives see Walter Phelps to Bro[?] Jared, c. 1908, ARC, UW-M, Milw SC 21.

[26] *History of Wisconsin*, II, 30. The *Sentinel's* colorful account of the line's first run appears in Austin, *The Wisconsin Story,* pp. 174-175. A copy of the "programme" of the day appears in August Derleth, *The Milwaukee Road* (New York: Creative Age Press, 1948), pp. 33-34.

[27] Letter of Charles I. Linsley to his father, cited in Austin, *The Wisconsin Story*, p. 177.

[28] *History of Wisconsin*, II, 30.

[29] *Report Made by Byron Kilbourn, Relating to a Settlement of the Flanders Fraud, Also a Report Relating to the Stock Subscriptions Made by J. L. Bean, Esq., Also a Brief History of the Flanders Fraud: Together with a Review of the Annual Report of the Directors of the Milwaukee and Mississippi R.R. Co. to the Stock Holders, January 11, 1853*. Kilbourn's defense was divided into four sections: report of the fraud (December 21, 1851), report of stock subscriptions (January 19, 1852), brief history of the fraud (November 1, 1852), and review of the annual report (January 17, 1853). It is interesting to note that Kilbourn used the "house divided" metaphor seven years before Abraham Lincoln did.

[30] *Ibid.*, 4.

[31] *The Railroads of Wisconsin, 1827-1937* (Railroad & Locomotive Historical Society, 1937), p. 27.

[32] Duckett, *Strong*, p. 118.

[33] Current, *History of Milwaukee*, 11, 33.

[34] *Milwaukee River*, p. 26.

[35] George G. Frederick, *When Iron Was King in Dodge County, Wisconsin, 1845-1928* (Mayville, Wis.: Mayville Historical Society, 1993), p. 55. A science teacher and local historian, Frederick did an admirable job of accumulating data and analyzing his subject matter. The account we present here follows the documented version he provides in the work cited above. See especially pp. 12, 54, 87, 91-92, 103-104, 123, 132.

[36] Derleth, *Milwaukee Road*, p. 234; Austin, *Milwaukee Story*, 42.

[37] At first the mining company's objective was to supply track for the La Crosse and Milwaukee, but a decade later when ore began to be extracted from the site, the goal broadened to include the iron needs of the American economy as a whole. British metal imports subsequently declined.

[38] E.C. Dixon, "Newport: Its Rise and Fall," *Wisconsin Magazine of History*, 25:4 (June 1942), passim.

[39] Passage from the *History of Columbia County* Cited in Dixon, p. 447.

[40] Bud Gussel, "Bailey Was Kilbourn Pioneer," *Historic Dells Country*, May 24, 1984, p 2. See also pp. 449, 453. Interview with G. Berquist, August 12, 1989. Writing in 1982, Kathy Walch took the view that "evidence of the intent of fraud seems never actually proven. Much that remains, however strongly implicating, is circumstantial.... The passing years seemed to have established the fact that the changes in location of both dam and bridge were due to reasonable causes with no intent to defraud." Walch concludes, "The complete

story of the tale of the dead city and the birth of another may never be known."
"A Tale of Two Cities," *Historic Dells Country*, I, No. 1, pp. 6, 13.

[41] Closing Exhibition of the Kilbournites at Kilbourn City, November 20, 1858. For One Day Only! Under the Tutelage, Guidance and Management of the Hon. Byron. Doors 0pen Precisely at Daylight. Performance to Commence at 9 A.M.

[42] Byron Kilbourn to P. Stroud, January 4, 1865, Stroud Papers, privately held by Bud Gussel.

[43] J. Bailey to P. Stroud, June 6, 1864, quoted in *Historic Dells Country*, May 25, 1984, p. 9. Mr. Gussel generously supplied the authors with copies of fourteen whole or partial letters between Kilbourn his local attorney and land agent, Stroud. This material deals primarily with real estate transactions and the early development of Kilbourn City. Reference to Byron's Kilbourn City holdings also appear in a ledger in the Bowman Papers, SHSW.

[44] Current, *History*, II, 15-16.

[45] John M. Bernd, "The La Crosse and Milwaukee Land Grant, 1856," *Wisconsin Magazine of History* 30 (December 1946), 142*ff.* Bernd's version of this complex story provides the background for this account.

[46] *Ibid.*, p. 143.

[47] Strong, p. 128. Strong's estimate of the value of the northwest land grant appears in Current, *History*, II, 246.

[48] *Doty,* pp. 339-340.

[49] Cited in Titus, *History of the Fox River Valley*, p. 327.

[50] "The La Crosse Grant," p. 145.

[51] *Report of the Joint Select Committee Appointed to Investigate into Alleged Frauds and Corruption in the Disposition of the Land Grant of the Legislature of 1856, And For Other Purposes* (Madison 1858), pp. 4-10.

[52] Cobb's testimony at the hearing of the joint select committee is cited in "The Question Box," *Wisconsin Magazine of History*, 5(1921-22), 210.

[53] *Strong*, p. 129.

[54] *Ibid.,* pp. 132-133.

[55] The cartoon appeared in *Harper's Weekly*, June 12, 1858 and is reprinted in *Strong* facing p. 129.

[56] Senate Journal, Vol. I, Wisconsin (January 1858), Governor's Message to the Legislature, January 14, 1858, p. 38.

[57] Duckett, *Strong*, pp. 134-135; Bernd, "The La Crosse Grant," p. 150.

[58] Duckett, *Strong*, p. 135.

[59] *Ibid.*, pp. 140-141. See also Kenneth W. Duckett, "Politics, Brown Bread,

and Bologna," *Wisconsin Magazine of History*, 36:3 (Spring 1953), 178*ff*.

[60] *Review of the Report Made by the Committee of Investigation to the Legislature of Wisconsin Relating to the Land Grant, Byron Kilbourn, Late President La Crosse & Mil. R.R. Co.*, Milwaukee, July 1858.

[61] *Ibid.*, p. 30.

[62] "The La Crosse Land Grant," pp. 145-146. The legislative investigation not only destroyed Kilbourn's public career but also affected the future of one of his associates; in the election of 1863, Henry L. Palmer, a La Crosse Company attorney, ran for governor on the Democratic ticket and was overwhelmingly defeated, in part because Republicans denounced him as the tool of "corruptionists." Merk, *Economic History*, pp. 256-257.

Epilogue

Byron Kilbourn wrote a family genealogical society that he came to Wisconsin because he "felt a strong desire to see it, with a view of repeating there what my father had once done in Ohio; viz., by early and judicious investments in its soil, to make an estate out of its settlement."[1] He did this, and a great deal more. He established Milwaukee's first newspaper and built Wisconsin's first railroad. He secured the territory's first land grant to build a canal to the Mississippi, and eighteen years later secured a second land grant to construct a rail line from Madison to Lake Superior. Although the waterway he planned to connect Milwaukee with the Rock River was never completed, a critical link in Milwaukee was, providing cheap water power for new industry. Kilbourn was a tireless champion of harbor improvement; the "straight cut" he recommended was the route later chosen to connect Lake Michigan and the Milwaukee River, the passage still in use today. He was twice elected Milwaukee's mayor, and missed becoming a U. S. Senator by a single vote. He donated the land for a city park and reservoir so that an emergency supply of water would always be available in case of fire. He also gave the city the land where the centrally located Milwaukee Auditorium now stands at North Sixth Street and West Kilbourn, along with land for a west side elementary school. In 1843 Kilbourn helped found a Masonic lodge. Later, he often served as its leader and provided a suitable meeting place for lodge meetings, acts which caused his brethren to name their organization in his honor.

Byron Kilbourn was a man who wore many hats. He was a surveyor and canal engineer, a land speculator and urban developer, a public official and his community's leading promoter. He was a venture capitalist with a sharp eye to the future. In moving to Milwaukee from Ohio, he risked all that he had saved and could borrow, and in the fierce competition that followed for land and leadership, he was determined to succeed. Succeed he did, amassing a sizable fortune and becoming the fifth wealthiest man in the state.[2] Intelligent, farsighted, energetic, and persistent, "no one did more to put Milwaukee on the map."[3]

But Kilbourn had many critics. Anyone who attempts as much as he did can expect them. Some people objected to the aggressive methods he used to advance the cause of Kilbourntown. They recalled the bridge over the Menominee River he had built to connect his town directly with the Chicago Road, thereby bypassing George Walker's southside settlement. Or they remembered the small tender *Badger* he had built, to meet ships in the outer harbor and transport freight and passengers to his dock at Chestnut Street, never stopping at Solomon Juneau's east side. Moreover, the copper plate map Kilbourn had ordered in Cincinnati gave a distorted view of reality, suggesting that the east side was largely an uninhabitable swamp, when in fact it was a thriving community as big as his own. Further, Kilbourn had ordered the roads in Kilbourntown to be built at an angle to those in Juneautown, resulting in Milwaukee's unusual river bridges we see today. Wisconsin farmers cursed the day they mortgaged their land to support a Kilbourn canal or railroad. But the deeds that concerned his critics the most involved his attempts to take control of the Milwaukee and Mississippi Railroad, his offer to subsidize Sherman Booth's newspaper in exchange for editorial support, and his efforts to win public and legislative support for his railroad in the La Crosse land grant case. For his part, Byron denied the first and third charges, and considered the second unobjectionable.

His opponents did not charge him with breaking the law. Instead, they objected to the methods he used to gain his ends. Some people called him a rascal or a scoundrel; some, a crook. But as Josiah Noonan, a shrewd contemporary, noted, "he was as honest as the law required."

The most controversial case of political influence in Wisconsin history involved the distribution of over $800,000 in railroad securities by Byron Kilbourn and his associates. Critics claimed the officials of the La Crosse and Milwaukee Railroad "bribed" the governor, state legislators of both parties, and important opinion leaders in exchange for their support. In response, Byron argued that the securities he distributed were not bribes at all, since most of Wisconsin's assemblymen and senators intended to support his bid all along. His gratuity to each of them, he said, was nothing more than standard business practice. He also pointed out that his leading competitor, William Ogden of the Chicago and North Western, used methods similar to his own while escaping opprobrium. Given the standards of the day, Kilbourn's behavior was remarkable more because of its scope than its nature. The prize he sought was the largest in the new state's history. A joint investigating committee took three months to hear his case – its managers taking care to see that his railroad rather than Ogden's received the lion's share of attention. At the end of the investigation, Byron paid no fine and spent no time in jail. But he lost his good name, and retired thereafter from public life. The *Milwaukee Sentinel*, along with other newspapers in the state, maintained that he failed to justify his actions in the La Crosse case. Then this same newspaper turned around and praised his plans for establishing a local university. As one student of the great engineering projects of the day put it, "So much good was going to come out of so comparatively little evil, it was generally felt the evil seemed a reasonable price to pay, and probably inevitable in any event."[4]

Whether you thought of Byron Kilbourn as a great man of vision or a great scoundrel depended upon the filter you used. Milwaukee businessman Daniel Wells, a Kilbourn contemporary, was a man who "was careful to guard his own financial reputation and those of his banks, yet he saw nothing wrong in buying the influence of legislators, and he shrewdly took advantage of any technicalities in state laws."[5] As the wife of Moses Strong put the matter in 1843, "There were not more than a hundred men in the territory who could not 'be bought by a little self interest or flattery or self love.'"[6]

At age thirty-one, Kilbourn left the employ of the Ohio Canal Commission because of crippling rheumatism. He was intermittently in poor health thereafter. In 1834, he told Micajah Williams of his difficulty in surveying townships in the cedar swamps of Manitowoc County. In 1840, a "severe affliction of the shoulder" caused him to board a steamer for Sandusky, Ohio, to seek the help of a resident surgeon. In 1861, the *Daily Wisconsin* reported that he was "lying dangerously ill at his residence" at Fourth and Wisconsin. At one point he was totally blind, but in time he did recover.[7]

After the Civil War ended, he and Henrietta traveled throughout the south, seeking warm weather and the medicinal benefits of hot springs in Arkansas. In 1868, they decided to move south permanently, choosing to live in Jacksonville, Florida. Jacksonville had been a "Union" city in the recent war and was about to experience a wave of prosperity. Byron invested in a 450-acre citrus ranch and moved much of his capital south to Atlanta, expecting to invest in new ventures in the New South. But he was crippled at the time and could move about only with difficulty. He died of a stroke in December of 1870, barely two years after he relocated there.[8]

Byron Kilbourn retired from public life in 1858 but he continued to pursue an active career in business right up until the time of his death twelve years later. As we noted in an earlier chapter, Kilbourn devoted much attention to his speculation in iron in Dodge County, particularly between the years 1864 and 1868. His involvement with the affairs of Kilbourn City preceded the outbreak of the Civil War and included the critical decision of where to locate a railroad bridge and dam. Byron founded the Kilbourn Manufacturing Company of Kilbourn City to facilitate the development of local industry through water power, much as he had earlier done in harnessing the Milwaukee River. While Byron never actually took up residence in Kilbourn City, he played a key role there, often acting through surrogates and land agents. He advanced funds necessary for the construction of a "Kilbourn Dam," carefully taking deeds on notes of obligation in return. As a careful student of the Wisconsin River Hydraulic Company explains, "in 1858... Kilbourn was given a mortgage on the land around the dam for a little over $1 thousand [dollars]. The following year he sued for non-payment plus interest, causing the property to be foreclosed on and sold at a sheriff's sale. It was purchased by Havens Cowles for $150, who it conveniently turns out was Kilbourn's nephew. Cowles then began to acquire a number of adjacent parcels – they eventually amounted to almost two hundred and thirty-six acres – which he sold for $1500 to his uncle in January of 1865. In this and other ways Kilbourn eventually acquired a total of eight hundred acres in the immediate area."[9] In Jacksonville, in 1868, Kilbourn invested in a large orange ranch and had plans for further investment in Florida at the time of his death.

A life-sized statue of Solomon Juneau, Milwaukee's first permanent settler, stands today on a bluff in Lake Park. Although a similar statue of Byron Kilbourn was designed in July of 1929, it was never erected on the boulevard known as Kilbourn Avenue, probably because of the economic depression that followed.[10] The relationship between these two founders varied over time. In the beginning, they cooperated with one another, exchanging parcels of land on either side of the Milwaukee River to fill out their spread. In the spring of 1836, Juneau and Martin even proposed to merge their interests with Kilbourn and Williams so the four could develop Milwaukee together, but the offer was turned down. Each man competed with the other between 1836 and 1839 in the race for new settlers. Both hoped to locate a courthouse, post office, and government land office on their side of the river; Juneau won on all three counts. But Kilbourn ordered the *Badger* constructed so he could bring newcomers directly to his dock and thus bypass the east side. And his efforts to advertise Kilbourn-town were more extensive and vigorous than his rival's. At times, partisans on both sides of the river loudly denounced their neighbors. But with the gradual recovery from the Economic Panic of 1837, tempers cooled, and Kilbourn and Juneau collaborated for the general good. Together they petitioned the territorial legislature to establish a single Town of Milwaukee, a request quickly granted. Both men could be counted upon to support such community advancement projects as the Milwaukee and Rock River Canal. Both provided financial support for a county agricultural society. Juneau was incapable of holding a grudge against anyone, and Kilbourn, once persuaded collaboration was in his best interest, quickly came aboard. The so-called "Bridge War of 1845" did pit forces on the two sides of the river against one another. East-siders and west-siders were sure their neighbors were unwilling to pay their fair share of bridge maintenance. But the "war" was more comic opera than live conflict. Kilbourntown, Juneautown, and Walker's Point each jealously guarded its own financial interests for many years after Milwaukee established a single government. When Milwaukee became a city in 1846, Juneau was elected mayor, and Kilbourn, a west-side alderman. When Juneau was unable to preside at a meeting, he asked Kilbourn to replace him. The truth is that the Ohio canal engineer and the French-Canadian fur trader were not bitter enemies; they competed with one another, to be sure, but they could also work in harmony when it suited their purposes to do so.

There is a common saying that the apple doesn't fall far from the tree. "A son is like his father" would, we think, be a logical extension of this idea. In what ways were James Kilbourn and his second son, Byron, alike? How did they differ from one another? Let us consider the record.

Both men were surveyors, and both exhibited energy and drive in establishing new towns. Both started from scratch, though Byron had the advantage of seven years of formal education and the Kilbourn name, a considerable asset in the central Ohio of the early nineteenth century. Land was the key to prosperity for both men; both were successful speculators in the regions in which they chose to settle. Both men founded newspapers to advertise their new towns, and both dreamed of creating new forms of transportation to increase the value of their holdings. In this last category, Byron was the more successful, creating Wisconsin's first railroad, and, with his short canal link, laying the basis for Milwaukee's future industry. Both men were elected to public office, though James' two terms in Congress were, all things considered, a more important achievement than Byron's being twice elected Mayor of Milwaukee. Both men were married twice and each had children by both wives. Both were loyal Masons. Both men had a strong sense of family pride: James reveled in his ancient English heritage, and Byron saw to it that his neighbors knew the facts about John Fitch, his inventive grandfather, who died before he was born.

Father and son differed in the matter of reputation, wealth, and community leadership. The Colonel maintained his good name throughout his career, but Byron was considered immoral by a number of his peers. James was devastated by the collapse of his Worthington Manufacturing Company in the aftermath of the War of 1812. Byron, on the other hand, became a wealthy man through the sale of real estate and his diverse interests in railroads, mining, and milling.

For almost half a century, James was the unquestioned leader of Worthington, Ohio, the community he founded. In contrast, Byron shared the limelight in Milwaukee with Solomon Juneau and George Walker. Both father and son were proud of their accomplishments, though Byron felt he achieved much more than his father had. The younger Kilbourn might well have been surprised to discover how much like his father he actually was.

James Kilbourn was five years old at the start of the Revolutionary War. Byron was eleven when the War of 1812 began. Neither saw action in battle, though James was elected colonel of his militia regiment in 1814. The story was different, however, for the next generation. Byron Hector Kilbourn, James' grandson and Byron's son, was twenty years old at the outbreak of the Civil War. He enlisted in Company D of the Third Wisconsin and was commissioned a second lieutenant. His regiment was organized by ex-Governor William Barstow in January of 1862. There were 78 men in young Kilbourn's company and he was third in the chain of command. His unit fought battles in both the eastern and western theaters of the war, including Bolivar, Winchester, Cedar Mountain, Second Bull Run, Antietam, Chancellorsville, Gettysburg, Chattanooga, and Atlanta. [11]

One final difference should be noted: James was reared in the revolutionary era of George Washington, John Adams, and Thomas Jefferson. Byron, on the other hand, fought to secure an estate in the early national period of Andrew Jackson, Martin Van Buren, and John Tyler. Both Kilbourns were largely self-made men, Byron having the greater impact in the long run.

In December of 1998, a local Milwaukee historical organization arranged to have Byron's remains removed from the Old City Cemetery at Jacksonville and reburied beside his wife, Henrietta, in the family plot at Forest Home Cemetery in Milwaukee. Byron Hector had planned to do this in 1887, but somehow the transfer was not undertaken until over a century later.[12] Whatever residents thought of Byron Kilbourn, he may well have been "the ablest man" in the city in his day.[13] One fact remains clear: he did all in his power to make Milwaukee great.

Endnotes

[1] Address to the Kilbourn Historical and Genealogical Society, August 20, 1854.

[2] Leo Soltow, *Patterns of Wealthholding in Wisconsin Since 1850* (Madison: University of Wisconsin Press, 1971), pp. 5-6, 31-33. See also federal census of 1860.

[3] John Gurda, "Rest in peace, Mr. Kilbourn, you character," *Milwaukee Journal-Sentinel*, January 3, 1999.

[4] David McCullough, *The Great Bridge* (New York: Simon and Schuster, 1972), p. 83.

[5] Dorothy J. Ernst, "Daniel Wells, Jr. -- Banker Extraordinary: A Case History of Banking Activities in Wisconsin and Minnesota, 1856-1858," *Minnesota History*, 40:3 (Fall 1966).

[6] Duckett, *Strong*, p. 59.

[7] B. Kilbourn to M. T. Williams, October 28, 1840, OHC, Williams Papers; I. Lapham to D. Lapham, November 2, 1840, MCHS, Lapham Papers, B4 F6; *Daily Wisconsin*, April 10, 12, 1861.

[8] Goodwin Berquist and Paul Bowers, "Byron Kilbourn's Last Years in Florida," *Milwaukee History*. 13:1 (Spring 1990), *passim*. Byron paid $850 for his property, a rock-bottom price. Three years later, his widow sold the property for $5,200.

[9] Rick Durbin, unpublished manuscript entitled "The Kilbourn Dam: A Tale of Many Hopes, Dreams, and Schemes," pp. 23-24, 1997.

[10] *Milwaukee Journal*, July 14, 1929.

[11] Frank Klement, *Wisconsin and the Civil War* (Stevens Point, WI: Worzalla Publishing Co., 1963), *passim*.

[12] *Milwaukee Journal-Sentinel*, November 20, 24, December 17, 1998; obituary of Henrietta Kerrick Kilbourn, *Milwaukee Sentinel*, July 2, 1887. Frank Matusinec of Historic Milwaukee, Inc., was the principal person responsible for returning Byron's remains to Milwaukee.

[13] Undated newspaper clipping, Milwaukee County Historical Society, newspaper file, Box 88.

Illustrations

Unless otherwise noted, all illustrations are from the collection of the Milwaukee County Historical Society. The following illustrations have been used with permission:

Page 1: Worthington Historical Society
Page 3: Ohio Historical Society
Page 4: Grand Lodge F. and A. M., Worthington, Ohio
Page 5: Ohio Historical Society
Page 46: State Historical Society of Wisconsin,
    WHi (X3) 17675
Page 74: State Historical Society of Wisconsin,
    WHi (X3) 45583
Page 76: Kilbourn Masonic Lodge
Page 86: Great Lakes Marine Collection of the
    Milwaukee Public Library / Wisconsin Marine
    Historical Society
Page 93: State Historical Society of Wisconsin
Page 128: State Historical Society of Wisconsin,
    WHi (X3) 1083
Page 145: State Historical Society of Wisconsin,
    WHi (X3) 18154
Page 148: State Historical Society of Wisconsin,
    WHi (X3) 1499
Page 157: *When Iron Was King* by George G. Frederick,
    c. 1993, reprinted with author's permission.
Page 158: *When Iron Was King* by George G. Frederick,
    c. 1993, reprinted with author's permission.
Page 160: Dells County Historical Society
Page 161: State Historical Society of Wisconsin, Bennett
    Collection, WHi (X3) 52682
Page 162: State Historical Society of Wisconsin,
    WHi (X3) 21075
Page 163: Dells County Historical Society
Page 164: Dells County Historical Society
Page 168: State Historical Society of Wisconsin,
    WHi (X3) 52683